AWESOME WOMEN ON THE MOVE PRESENTS...

WHAT IT IS LIKE BEING A

DR. TENARIA DRUMMOND-SMITH

With 24 CO-AUTHOR WOMEN

Awesome Women On The Move
WHAT IT IS LIKE BEING A WOMAN

HOV Publishing a division of HOV, LLC.
www.hovpub.com / hopeofvision@gmail.com

Cover Design: HOV Design Solutions
Editor/Proofreader: Jeff Smith and HOVP Editing Services

Write the author Tenaria Drummond-Smith at: tds@awesomewomenonthemove.org
For more information about special discounts for bulk purchases,
please contact Tenaria Drummond-Smith or hopeofvision@gmail.com

Paperback ISBN: 978-1-955107-97-6
eBook ISBN: 978-1-955107-96-9
Library of Congress Control Number:

10 9 8 7 6 5 4 3 2

Printed in the United States of America

Endorsement

Dr. Lenora Peterson

Dr. Tenaria Drummond Smith is one who holds valuable things for many others, all the time. Her talents and energies are used to serve others spiritually, helping them grow in their gifts. She also knows how to share with others her greatest example of teaching in servanthood. By being a leader, her purpose is to help other women grow.

Goodwill Ambassador Dr. Lenora Peterson-Maclin

Dr. Lenora Peterson-Maclin
Goodwill Ambassador / Chief Executive at GIA-
National Volunteer Community Service
A PO Box 2596, Duluth, Georgia 30096
P 404-585-0984
M WhatsApp: USA/ 14047974062
E womanofgodforever@gmail.com
W giaadvocateuniversity.com

AWESOME WOMEN ON THE MOVE PRESENTS...

WHAT IT IS LIKE BEING A

Introduction

I decided to do a book for women to express who they are as women, but in a way where each woman felt free to express themselves through personal stories of what their truth was and is. As a woman, I believe we should all come together and be with one accord, but that is not always the case. We know that women do not always get along, but I want to be living proof and make that a false claim. The true issue is that there are women who do not like themselves, so it becomes almost impossible for them to like others.

With the vision of this women's book, I believe it will be a spiritual and emotional release. As women, we can take a look at ourselves and how view other women. Despite all our trials and struggles, we want better. We can do better for ourselves without passing judgment against our sisters. We can encourage one another to help build each other up. I am very clear about the purpose of this book because I know that women will identify with these stories through things that women experience. But through it all and despite what I have gone through, I give God the praise: "I will praise thee; for I am fearfully and wonderfully made: marvellous are thy works; and that my soul knoweth right well." (Psalm 139:14)

Dr. Tenaria Drummond-Smith

@AwesomeWomenOnTheMove
e: tds@awesomewomenonthemove.org

Content

CHAPTER 1

Unapologetic

TENARIA DRUMMOND-SMITH

I like to think of myself as a very humble but confident woman who knows what she wants and how to work hard to get what I want. I thank God for giving me parents who encouraged me to be the best that I can be, never settling and always going higher. Today, their encouraging words have really helped me to be a woman with unshakable faith and who knows that all things are possible. I do not have to look like or act like someone else. I do not have to be what society portrays me to be because of things like my hairstyle, my body type, or the color of my skin. What I have found is that people who question me about any of these things are usually the ones who have issues their own selves. Just on questions about my hairstyle alone, I have had a journey that is worth me writing about and sharing.

I never thought of myself as an average woman because I always had visions and dreams of doing extraordinary things in my life. I knew that I was different because I never really wanted to do the things my family or friends did. I remember spending time looking around and shopping at boutique stores in Greenwich Village in Manhattan (New York City). I used to wear colorful box braids and cornrows for a different look. In the late 70's and 80's, I mostly wore my hair in cornrows if my mother did not take me and my older sister Parama (Pam) to the hairdresser to get a press and curls. My mother never put relaxers in our hair, but she did use a hot straightening comb to give our hair length and texture when styling for special occasions.

In January 1977, my family and I watched the TV series "Roots". Afterwards, I had an idea of wearing my hair in a style that was different from how I wore it, which was called a mushroom style. I asked my mother if I could use one of her long pony tails to help me style my hair. She agreed and cut it into sections to help grab it easily to add to my own hair. I parted my hair and braided the loose hair in with my own. I did not do a cornrow. I box-braided my entire head. At that time, I called it adding extensions. I did this because I wanted to create different styles and the loose hair helped to give my hair length. Today, that style is called box braiding and it is very popular, but at that time no one was wearing their hair with added extensions. I did not see anybody in my school or in my neighborhood doing what I did. I got a lot of complements, but I also had people calling me names, like "fake hair" and just about everything else you could think of. I was really confused about it. I could not understand why adding extra hair to my head had anything to do with anyone else. And let me be clear: the name calling came from girls and boys who were older than me. I was in junior high school, and I remember entering the school building one day to go to my gym class. When I walked into the gym, I had a lot of stares. They were probably wondering how in the world my hair grew so fast overnight! My gym teacher walked over to me and said, "Tenaria, I didn't know your hair could grow like that, but I love it!" I thanked him and took my spot on the gym floor. Meanwhile, the other students kept looking at me in shock and, of course, one of my friends tried to touch my hair. I told them all I would not mind them looking at my hair, but I did mind them trying to touch me. I already had it made up in my mind that I was going to keep wearing my hair like that because I did not see anybody around me wearing it the way that I did. This gave me a sense of boldness, and the name calling only motivated me to be more creative and dream up other ways of styling my hair. After the shock wore off and my hairstyle started becoming popular in school and around the neighborhood, I turned hair braiding into a business. I was not just a young student. I was a young woman being sought after to create hairstyles with extensions. I mastered my hair braiding craft so well that people could look at someone's braids and know whether I did them or not. I really enjoyed the fact that I was a young trendsetter in Bushwick, Brooklyn. I was known as "the hair braider from Madison Street"!

Since I was making money from this, I decided to open my own store, but I needed to be licensed to do other things besides braiding. I attended Barbizon Beauty School in downtown Brooklyn. I was so excited to begin my classes. I wanted to be licensed in a hurry. When I got there for enrollment, I was impressed to see that the students were diverse, and I wanted to network with young women from different backgrounds. On the first day of class, I left an hour early to get there because I did not want to be late. As I walked down the street to the school, I saw a bunch of girls hanging out in front of the building, smoking cigarettes. I figured that I might as well get my last smoke in because who knew when I might be able to get a break? A girl walked up to me and asked if I had another cigarette. I did, so I gave her one. Once we were done, it was time for us all to head to class. We were broken up into two groups, A and B. I was in group A, but it looked like group B had more people in it. I have no idea why, but it just did. I noticed that in group B, many of the girls were linked with the girls they came in with. The instructor asked if we could all introduce ourselves to one another, if we had not done so already. I walked across the room to introduce myself to everyone. Not many of the girls did this, but I thought maybe they were introverts, and this was fine by me. I noticed some girls in group B stared at me like I did something wrong to them. I did not let that bother me. I was not there for friendship. I was there to get licensed. As the day went on, I asked a lot of questions about the benefits of becoming a licensed cosmetologist. The instructor thought I asked some good questions. After this, we picked up our supplies so we could do demos on wig heads. When I walked to the back of the room where the supplies were, two girls were lingering, as though they were waiting for me to come near them. When I went to grab a wig head, one of them tried to brush up against me. I thought to myself, "Here we go again with someone trying to start trouble with me without even getting to know me!" When class was almost over, but before we were dismissed, our instructor handed each student a large black Barbizon tote bag with books, hair supplies, and a wig head. I thought about how we had to drag that big thing around back and forth every day. Class was over, good night. The next day, it was the same thing with those girls staring at me like they had a problem with me. I kept my distance.

But one day in class, about two weeks into the semester, I had this feeling that something was going to happen. By this time, we were learning how to do finger waves. I set up my wig head, setting lotion, rollers, and bobby pins. We watched our instructor demonstrate how the process was done. When the bell rang for a class break, I asked if I could have a word with her outside. I told her that I believed there were two girls in group B who seemed to have a problem with me. When we both came back into the room, there was setting lotion spilled all over my desk and books. When the instructor asked the class who did it, of course no one admitted to doing it. One of the girls who I was cool with later informed me that she heard some girls were planning on jumping me after class. For whatever reason—I could not even tell you today—I went to the school office to arrange to have my parents pick me up from school. After they arrived and as we drove by the building, we saw those girls at the bus stop where I normally caught the bus going home. My parents decided that I was no longer going to attend that school anymore.

In 2002, my mother passed away. I got hurt on my city job and was released from it. I wanted to do something different with my life. I no longer wanted to do hair or wear my hair in braids. I was looking to do something that I never did before. My husband encouraged me to cut my hair. When he told me, I thought about the time when I once mentioned to my mother how I was considering cutting my hair. She had no idea that my intention was to shave most of my hair off. She told me she did not think that I should do it. Months after my mother passed away, I found the courage to be bold again. My husband took my hand and told me that I looked beautiful. The barber handed me the mirror and I started to weep because my mother told me not to do it, but I did it anyway. At that point, I felt free and empowered because of all the compliments I got later on that day. I thought to myself about how it seemed like I got more compliments than when I had long hair! I decided to keep my head shaved because it was really easy for me to maintain.

I remember one year when my husband and I, along with a friend, decided to take a drive to a Benny Hinn crusade in Pennsylvania. When we got there, the lines were long because people came from all over. We were so excited to see the power of God move through people. We had a casual conversation with four people who were near us on the line waiting to get into the building. We all wound up being seated next to each other once we got into the auditorium. After the crusade was over, we decided to stay in touch with each other. Before leaving the building, we stopped by the restrooms. The line to get into the women's restroom went way out into the main floor. As I spoke with some women on the line with me, they told me how beautiful I looked with my shaved head. One woman who spoke to me then waved at her friend to come over by us. I noticed that her friend had a pink scarf wrapped around her head. It looked like she might have lost her hair due to chemotherapy. The woman who I spoke with started rubbing my back and told me that everything was going to be alright. I told her that I was fine and despite what it might have looked like, I did not come to the crusade for being sick. I came because I wanted to see how God might use Benny Hinn to work miracles, signs and wonders. After explaining that my head was shaved by choice, I told the woman's friend that I was sorry for her having to battle with cancer and prayed that she would be well in the name of Jesus. Even today, I have people assume that because my head is shaved, I must be battling cancer myself. The truth is that for some women, that might the case, but that is not for every woman's case. There are women who may have alopecia. It taught me about why people must use discernment in their approach to folks. Apart from how I responded, another woman might not have been as nice. After I used the restroom, I walked out and never looked back at those women. I had never been approached about my appearance in that way. It felt like that woman used her friend and her friend's condition as a way of trying to make me feel better about a condition that did not apply to me. African and African-American women have been wearing shaved and bald heads for who knows how long. When I shaved my head, I embraced the look and feel. Some women feel that hair and wigs make them feel beautiful. I have no problem with any woman who chooses to wear wigs and weaves to make themselves look and feel the way they want to. I have no problem with anyone wearing their hair in ways that are suitable for them. It is none of my business. I think this one of the biggest problems women deal with most: always worrying about what some other women are doing or not doing.

From woman to woman, I believe that we can do so much better in how we speak to and treat each other. I believe that we should learn from and help uplift one another. I would like to see more of us having real sisterhood. The word of God says:

> *"For thou hast possessed my reins: thou hast covered me in my mother's womb. I will praise thee; for I am fearfully and wonderfully made: marvellous are thy works; and that my soul knoweth right well. My substance was not hid from thee, when I was made in secret, and curiously wrought in the lowest parts of the earth. Thine eyes did see my substance, yet being unperfect; and in thy book all my members were written, which in continuance were fashioned, when as yet there was none of them.*
>
> *Psalm 139:13-16*

I love everything about being the woman God created me to be. It is not always easy dealing with other women, but I have come to realize that there are so many issues that women have gone through, or are going through. I thank God for helping me realize that I can take the name calling, even when it hurts, because it showed me where my strength would come from. That strength would help me do what he called me to do. I am so happy that I do not allow people to try to work my situation out when they have no place to do that. That applies to my hairstyle and everything else about me. I have been approached many times about my look, especially by church-going women who keep talking about "a woman's glory", but I know that I do not have to explain myself. I love it, and I love myself. That is all that really matters.

CHAPTER 2

Becoming My Own

JACQUELENE SCRUGGS

I am very thankful to God for being a strong black woman. Women have so many hats to wear and so many roles to play. Women must be powerful through childbirth, discrimination, sexism, rape, wrongful accusation, and abuse. Being a woman can be rewarding and challenging at the same time. One of my challenging life experiences has made me to be the strong black woman that I am today. When I was younger, I thought I could outsmart life. I thought I could have sexual intercourse without using a condom and not get pregnant. When I ended up getting pregnant, I was so upset with myself. I thought to myself, "Now what am I going to do?" I was not working, and neither was my boyfriend. I had to tell my parents. I knew they were going to be disappointed in me, and they were. I told my boyfriend that I did not know what I was going to do, so he tried to help me figure it out. He said everything was ok because I did not have to keep my pregnancy. In the meantime, he went with me to my doctor's appointments. Two months before the baby was due, I found out he cheated on me with my friend. I was devastated. I decided to break up with him. He apologized and wanted to get back with me, but I would not take him back. Not only did he cheat on me, but he cheated on me with my close friend. With these two things happening at the same time, I really went through it. My blood pressure was all over the place. My feet were swollen. I was depressed and scared. I had thoughts that something could happen to my baby because of my health, especially since I was so close to my due date.

Thank God for letting my baby boy be born in good health! But I knew his father was incapable of taking care of him. Not only was he not working, but he also was not supportive and could not care less about his son, me, or anything else. I had to put my big girl pants on and I started taking care of our child on my own. I made my bed and now I had to lie in it. At that point, I had to apply for government assistance just to get by because finding a job was hard. I was hurt, embarrassed, and ashamed that I had to even resort to getting help from the government. All those feelings had me spiraling out of control. I felt like I should not have to raise my son by myself. I was worried because I had a baby boy and his father refused to be in his life. As my son got older, I eventually had the chance to return to school. It was very hard to juggle going to school and taking care of my son by myself, all at the same time. When I got home from school, I made sure my son was taken care of. I made sure he was bathed and fed before I started studying, because of the time I was getting home, I usually ended up finishing around eleven at night. Things became so overwhelming that I had to drop out of school. I thought it was best to look for a job to better support my son. My father knew I needed a job, so he pulled a few strings to help me land a city job as an HRA (Human Resources Administration) Police Officer. It was such a good job and I really enjoyed working there. My duty was to patrol and protect the area where HRA checks were made. I was so happy to finally be able to provide for my son. I worked there for about nine years, but around the fourth year, I met a handsome electrician. When we met, I knew in my heart that he was different from other men I dealt with in the past. One day when I was on my way to lunch, he came over to me and asked me if I was saved. I told him that I was and I asked him how did he know. He said he could tell because of the way I carried myself. I was impressed by how he even knew I was a Christian. He asked me for my phone number because he did not think he would return to the location where I was working.

That weekend, he flew out for his parents' fiftieth wedding anniversary. When he returned, he ended up returning to the same location where I was working and asked me out on a date. He was a perfect gentleman. When he picked me up, he opened the car door for me. He made me feel so special, and even pulled my chair out for me. We went to a very nice seafood restaurant. I ordered a shrimp and pasta dinner, while he ordered steak and potatoes. I ate steak from his plate, and he tasted shrimp from my plate. We really had a beautiful connection. After we ate, we went for a walk in the park. We sat on a bench and talked for a long time about life, just getting to know each other. We embraced each other. He left me very impressed by bringing me back home by ten o'clock. I was so impressed that I went out on another date with him. On the day when we made things official, he took me to a Broadway play. I never knew how beautiful and classical play could be. I liked him so much that I knew he was the one for me. I was so happy to be with him because he treated me like a queen. I knew if the opportunity came, I would spend the rest of my life with him. That opportunity came when he asked my father for my hand in marriage. My father agreed. My parents loved him and thought he was a true gentleman. They believed in their hearts he was truly the one for me.

We were engaged for six months. This time in my life was like a breath of fresh air. I enjoyed every minute of it. We had a long talk about the love we had for each other. I felt that in marriage, we should be as one, and equally yoked in the Lord. A family that prays together stays together. Two weeks after we spoke about that, he was baptized in the name of Jesus and filled with the Holy Ghost. He turned his life over to God, and his mother was so happy because she had already turned her life over. I was even happier to start a new life with someone I loved and could build life together with on a spiritual level. We had a beautiful wedding. I was so happy to be marrying my soulmate.

I thank God for having more children a few years after we were married. They were all raised up in church, baptized and filled with the Holy Ghost. I instilled in them to keep God first in everything, and to be God-fearing. They are not bad children, but as they grew up, they went out and did not always do the right things. I am still thankful that I never had to visit them in jail. I am also thankful to God for the relationship that my children have with me. We are always able to talk about anything. I am always there for them whenever they need to talk, even if they call me at two or three in the morning. Whenever they tell me about things they did that were not good, I never judge them. We are human, and we make mistakes. I have always been honest with my children about things I did when I was younger, including having unprotected sex and getting pregnant. I did not want them making the same kinds of mistakes I did.

I talked to them about staying safe by using contraception and using condoms to avoid diseases like HIV/AIDS. Even if I had to buy them or get them from a clinic myself, I always made sure they were equipped with condoms. Some people thought I was crazy because it was almost as if I was telling my children to go out and have sex, but that was not what I was doing. They were going to do what they were going to do anyway, and if that was the case, I just wanted them to take precautions. I did not want another child brought into the world and not have both parents be ready to take care of them. I did not want them to be part of the statistics that African Americans are labeled under. I did not want them to repeat my mistake.

I pray every day, because things in today's world are so bad, prayer is always essential. I am fearful that anything can happen to my children because of the color of their skin. They have to work harder than others just to be equal, and their survival is a matter of life and death. They can be singled out and accused of doing things they did not do. Always looking over their shoulders, they have to make sure they walk a straight line and not draw attention to themselves. The justice system makes the end results unfair for the black culture. As women, we are fighting hard to make changes in this world. Before the women's rights movement, there was a time when women were not able to have a voice. We could not vote, we could not own property, and could not serve in the military. It is hard to believe how women were so limited in what we were allowed to do, knowing that in the eyes of the Lord, we are all equal. But through the same Lord, we can do those things that he called us to do. We are strong and have to fight to make change. We still have work to do.

I am so thankful to God for the work he did in me, and for what he did for me. He kept me well and brought me through many obstacles. I thank God that I have come a long way. I have an everlasting love for my family. God is always there for me, and He is the reason why I made it. I have become my own Woman.

CHAPTER 3

Strength Of A Woman

SOPHIA L. GREENE

No one could prepare you for the elements of being a woman. This title takes on its own dimensions of emotions and responsibilities. No two women's experiences are the same, yet as women, we have many similarities. We are equipped enough to be a support system for a sister while tending to our own wounds and pain. As little girls, we enter this world with innocence and curiosity. We see the world as a big playground that is here to cater to our needs and nurture our hearts. We get excited. We yearn for stability and love in the home, and we depend on parents to nurture that environment. It is crucial that we are able to latch onto that period of breastfeeding while enjoying the warmth of the touch of mom (it is the substitute of the umbilical cord). We feel a sense of safety in each heartbeat as we fall asleep in a world that feels so safe. Dad speaks to mom with softness and a love that helps stabilize the calmness of the home. With this, that innocent princess is able to enjoy all the reassurance that was planned for her, and there will be no interruption of peace in her world. That princess feels safe that she will be able to grow and excel at a young lady's pace. This fairytale life sounds beautiful. We all hoped our stories began and stayed that way until we were prepared for adulthood, but most of our safety nets are disrupted by the time we finish breastfeeding; or even before we exit the womb. Some things change the trajectory of a woman's future, especially if she is not loved properly during infancy. She no longer grows with balance and joy. Now she operates from fear and a distrust that affects her whole being as a woman. It affects every atmosphere she enters.

There is a sense of security about family. My mom told me about her childhood. When she was seven years old, her mother put her on a train and gave her instructions to where she had to get off the train in another district. That train ride would take more than two hours. That safety net got shifted without conversation, and she was thrown into a new environment. My mom said when every weekend came, she watched and waited, hoping that her mother would return to get her. That wait lasted for eight years. Please know that I am talking about the early sixties, when we had no home phones or cell phones to stay connected. I cannot imagine what went through my Mom's mind; let alone what she thought as a seven year old child. Not knowing if she would see her mom again, or if the stop that she was instructed to get off was the right stop, or if someone would be there to collect her. Situations like these can rock your foundation as a child. They can stay with you until you grow into a woman. When a young girl feels unsafe in their home/family, she goes out in the world not trusting much and thinking she has to depend on herself. When my grandmother removed that safety blanket from underneath my mom's feet, it changed the way my mom looked at the world.

When I hear and see the strength of women, I see pain wrapped in courage. Personally, 1996 was a challenging time for me. Not only did I lose my dad to gun violence in the streets of Brooklyn, New York, but I was also pregnant with my second child at the same time. I already had a twelve year old son from a relationship I left, deciding it was not what I wanted to raise my child in. After burying my dad, I found myself preparing to raise my two children alone. I lost my home, and being too physically and mentally exhausted to work, this resulted in me being homeless in the America for the second time. After house hopping every night, I decided to go to the homeless shelter that was recommended to me, only to be turned down by the shelter twice. After going to the shelter for the third time, I was told to go to the welfare office and get a social worker so that I could have some type of income to be eligible for the shelter system. Finally, I was accepted and placed into the shelter system for single moms and children. I lived in a shelter for eight months, and my second child was born in the shelter system. Looking back twenty-four years ago, my son changed seven schools in eight months before we were settled into a stable shelter facility. Those eight months were a time of strength-building. Those eight months were my total dependence on God's mercy and grace. Those eight months taught me patience.

To me, being a woman is learning to how to be reduced to dirt so that we can be rebuilt into immovable rock of strength. We can do all things through Christ who strengthens us. It is the strength of a woman. Being a woman carries so much responsibility, such as walking with a child in hand and simultaneously walking with pain in your heart. Not skipping a beat, she supports and encourages a soul sister or a soul brother. Being a woman is a treasure and gift from God. We are entrusted with life and life lessons because God knows we are capable of this responsibility. Psalm 46:15 confirms that God is with a woman every waking day of her life. With that reassurance, we can have great delight in the promises of God and the ability to handle all the responsibilities that await us. Proverbs 31:16-21 speaks of the strength of a woman and all she can do by walking through her strength. One of the characteristics of being a woman is her emotional being. She carries a heart which is connected to her emotions, allowing her to feel other people's pain. She is able to exercise compassion and reach out to support them in all the ways that she is capable of. From creation, we are introduced to women who embody love and empathy. We watch and listen to these women exercise charity. Mother Teresa was one of those women who lived their life helping the needy and impoverished. Even though all women will not have this calling to dedicate their lives to the underserved, I say with conviction to trust and believe that there is a Mother Theresa within most women. It is one of the reasons why women do what they do.

Women are versatile, skilled in multitasking and nurturers by nature. Maybe that is why God made women to be life bearers. Women want to love and protect. We enjoy taking care of the nest. Women show love in their cooking, combing their children's hair, and in ways that can be taken for granted. All her love is on display through these chores. A woman loves deeper and harder because she has more depth and is more soulful than her counterpart; but of course, there are exceptions to the rule. We do know that there are women who are cold and callous, but we will focus on the majority of the soulful women who breathe love and exhale forgiveness so they can love from their core. A woman makes the home softer and more pleasant when she is loved correctly. She turns a house into a home so all who dwell inside feel warmth and serenity. What can compare to the hands of a woman when she knows what she carries? The womb of a woman is designed to carry the weight of new life to nourish it to full term while walking with grace. She does this while taking care of business with her family and lending her shoulder to cry on.

Woman, "womb-man", superhuman, teacher, queen, servant, counselor, therapist, cook, domestic helper, nurse, comforter, confidant, trusted friend, sister. Take your pick. No one wears the many hats of a woman. The *awesome* woman. What a gift and honor it is to be all that! Who am I to be embodied with all these jewels? Someone chose me! Yes, me! Yes, you! Someone said we are the vessel of love, truth, compassion, and empathy. God said we are capable of carrying all these titles simultaneously with pain. The art of being a woman is being a painting that is never completed. The form that represents a woman's soul has not been fully colored. The strength of a woman has no gage. It has unlimited measurement. Depending on what life throws at her, a woman can always go deeper and higher. She carries super strength in adversity. If you disbelieve me, catch a woman in motion when her child is in danger. A woman will run into a burning house to save her child without a thought. She leads not only with her head, but also with her heart.

The essence of a woman is the endless air we breathe. Proverbs 31:25 speaks of a woman's strength, and I cannot help but compare this verse to real life scenarios. Judith (my realtor) buried her husband and her mom within a six-month period, and she did it with dignity and strength. Cymbal (my soul sister) has a son who had a near-death experience that put him into a coma. She went to the ICU and prayed over her son daily. Even though doctors suggested that she pull the plug, she kept pleading the blood of Jesus over her son's life. He came out of that coma six months later. Claudius, her son, is walking, talking and taking care of all his personal needs. Strength surrounds this woman. My mother Callis was a single mother of two children. She used all her savings to purchase a home. She had no idea where her first mortgage payment would come from, but with courage and strength, she trusted God in faith. My grandmother Ikolyn told me when she was pregnant and lived with her child's father, they had a conflict where he took the roof off the house while it was raining. Not knowing where life would take her, she packed up her stuff and vowed not to live in another man's residence. In strength, she walked away. It reminds me of when my father was murdered, and I was pregnant and left homeless with an eleven-year-old child. Twice turned away by a homeless shelter. The strength, resilience, and persistence that I am wrapped in kept me going. Sometimes a woman will walk through a valley of darkness, but her strength shows the flow of a woman's rhythm. The strength of a woman never runs out because as she wakes up every day, she is ready to obtain a refill from her Creator to do what she was born to do. Nothing compares to the strength of a woman.

CHAPTER 4

A Different World

THERESA BYRD

Ever since I could remember, the rules were different for girls and boys. When the girls went outside to play, we had to stay close to the house, but the boys could go down the block. But we all had to be back in front of the house when the streetlights came on. My grandmother always sat in the front yard watching. In the summer, she would let us play in front of the house just a little longer. The summers were hot. When we went outside to play, the boys went in the street to play football or stick ball. The girls played hopscotch or double dutch on the sidewalk. After we finished playing, we all sat on the stoop. The boys could sit on the ground at the curbside. Once a week, the street was blocked off so the boys could open up the fire hydrant and we all could get wet. The boys stood over the hydrant with a can opened on both sides so they could shoot water on everyone. The adults did not let the girls do it though. We still had a good time.

On rainy days, both boys and girls were allowed to bring two friends into the house with adult supervision. The boys played electric football game upstairs in their bedroom. Their friends were allowed to go up with them, but the girls and their company had to play games at the kitchen table. Sometimes we would all get together to play a game like Monopoly. We learned how to buy properties, make profit, and sell before we went bankrupt. The game was very profitable because it gave everyone a sense of ownership. Sometimes it seemed like the game lasted forever. What counted the most was that everyone, boys and girls, came together with one accord. At that moment, there was no difference. We were just children having fun, playing a board game on a rainy day and sharing a lot of laughter.

One day, the boys came outside with a lot of material. They had nails, a hammer, a wooden milk crate, some two-by-four wood slabs, and old skate, a rope, and two wheels. All the girls sat on the stoop to watch them work. Whenever they ran into problems, an older brother came out to help. The boys worked hard on their project. By the time they finished, they had themselves a go-cart and a scooter. Now they had two things to share. When the girls saw the boys ride, we wanted to ride too. The boys decided to share the go-cart and scooter with us so we could all have fun...until an adult came outside and stopped everything. The adult said that the toys belonged to the boys, and for us girls to go play hopscotch or jump rope with each other. We did not understand why.

Summer ended, and it was time to go back to school. As we got into the swing of things, it was around Thanksgiving when our teacher gave us candy sale packages to take home. I gave the big white envelope to my mother, and when she looked inside, I did too. There were pictures of different types of candies and cookies but the thing that caught my eye was the booklet with different prizes to choose from. With my mother's help, I was able to sell things over the weekend. Sometimes my uncle or a male cousin would go with me from door to door. My mother helped more by taking the package to sell things at work, but my dad ordered a bunch of things from me just to keep me from going out with other little children. The boys went out on their own, even going alone to the projects a couple blocks down the street from us. Once we got to junior high school, they were able to get a paper route in the area, but this was not possible for the girls. We made our money doing things like helping our aunts with their babies or making runs to the corner store. Again, the boys and girls had different rules.

When we were teenagers, we liked to play hot peas and butter. The rules consisted of a person hiding a rope for the other players to find. Whoever found the rope chased the other players down to try and hit somebody. Everybody ran to base before getting caught, but the first person to get hit was the next person to hide the rope. Sometimes this game brought tears to many eyes. At times, kids tried to hide their feelings. While we played this game, everybody wanted to be Mr. Tough Guy. There was not a boy who would not give this game a shot. Even the girls tried to act tough and begged to play. The boys just laughed and told us to move out of their way, but sometimes they gave in. If an adult came outside or walked by while this game was going on, everybody stopped playing. All the girls had to stop playing right away. As we got a little older, we could leave the block and play in the park down the street. The girls always had to travel in twos. The rules changed: we now had a curfew, but it was not as late as the boys was. We also had different curfews for weekdays and weekends. Being an older teenager now, I was able to go to parties. Whenever the females went to a party, a male took us to and from the party. He checked out the surroundings. Sometimes he stayed, or he came back later to pick us up.

My grandmother was a housewife who did all the cooking. She assigned chores and we rotated them on a weekly basis. The girls' chores were to wash the dishes and clean up the kitchen completely. The boys' chore was taking out the garbage and replacing it with a new bag. Everyone had to keep their room clean. The males did not have as many chores as the females inside the house. When fall and winter came around, being a female worked in my favor. The males had the bigger responsibility in the chore department. In the fall, they had to rake leaves daily. On snow days, they had to shovel, spread rock salt on the ground, and always check to make sure there was no ice on the ground in front of the house. This is one of the times I felt like the rules between females and males made sense. Then came the time when fathers would have "the talk" with the males about the birds and the bees. Our mothers kept everything a big secret from us, except in the area of hygiene. In school, we had a hygiene class where they taught us the basics as well. By senior year in high school, the males no longer had too much of a curfew to follow; however, the females were pushed to the limit because we were so busy.

Since I am an only child, my dad chauffeured me around or had someone do it for him. I never thought about getting my driver's license. It was never on the top of my list. Even when trips and family functions came up, my dad continue to chauffeur us around. As time went by, he started pushing the idea of me getting my license. As I think about it, he never put me behind the wheel of his car to see if I was even interested in driving at all. When the guys were with him in the car, he let them drive regardless of them not having a license or even a learner's permit. As long as he was in the car, he let them drive. I guess it made a difference in how the guys were interested and excited about getting behind the wheel of a car. I decided to get my learner's permit. I took the five-hour class and paid for some driving lessons. My dad decided to send a few male family members my way to help. They came with his non-power steering 1979 Pontiac Bonneville for me to use for additional driving lessons. The funny thing about all this is that it did not matter to me if my dad let the guys drive his car long before he let me. I never wanted to do it at that time, but I am grateful that my dad encouraged me.

Now I am an adult with so many more new friends added to my circle. My life schedule has changed. I needed a job. I checked newspapers, went to job agencies, and applied for exams. I looked at job titles, their duties, and requirements. As I process things during my job search, something caught my eye. Some job listings state needing men only. I saw this before along the way, but there was no time for me to stop. Life was moving on, and so was I. At times, I worked at places where the salary was different for men and women doing the same job. Some companies kept women and men in separate departments so they could pay them differently. But things began to change. Barriers were knocked down little by little. I am beginning to step into myself more each day. There are more avenues for me to take. In the beginning, all I saw was the different sets of rules for boys and girls. Now seeing through a woman's eyes, I see how those rules are still applied. Even in my life. My grandfather once told me that I have more opportunity than he did in his days. He told me to take advantage of everything I could, and that I did not need to compromise myself unnecessarily. As the story of my life grows, so do I. The one big thing I owe myself in this life is to always believe in myself. While going down memory lane, even from kindergarten years up until now, I realize how the men and women in my life live by different rules.

We are expected to even cry out for help differently. After going over my life and the different rules I dealt with as a woman, this scripture came to me: "[1]I will lift up mine eyes unto the hills, from whence cometh my help. [2]My help cometh from the LORD, which made heaven and earth." (Psalms 121: 1-2) As I grew up, my family was the biggest part of my village. We had God in our lives as a family, though I did not know him for myself. But as I got older and trouble started coming my way, it seemed like there was nowhere for me to turn. I did not know how to express the thoughts that were locked up inside me because boys and girls had different rules. I did not know how to reach out for help, but something I had in my favor was being taught how to pray by my mother, my grandparents, and my great-grandparent. When I was a little kid, they made sure I knew the Lord's Prayer. At that time in my life, I was in a dark tunnel with no light to be seen. I heard crying. After a while, I realized it was me crying. Before I knew it, I started praying and crying for help. All the thoughts and feelings I kept bottled up came out. I asked God for peace of mind and to take away my pain. He let me see light at the end of the tunnel. God carried me when I could not walk for myself. Through all my trials and tribulations, God has been guiding me through and loving me non-stop. My God is awesome.

CHAPTER 5

What Momma Said

VON BRAND

Being a woman surely is not easy, but somebody has to do it. I can still hear the words of my mother telling us eight of us children to stay children for as long as we could. When we became adults, there was no turning back. Man, oh man, do you know how right she was? Growing up in a household with seven other siblings was challenging at times, but I must say that I truly had my share of fun. My childhood was fairly good, and I really do not have any real complaints. I grew up in a very strict environment. It seemed like we were in church 24/7. You might be asking yourself, "How did that make you a woman?" Well, I am glad that you asked. Just stay with me. Read on and I will tell you.

You see, growing up in a household where our mom's faith was Apostolic Pentecostal left us with no real choices of our own. Joshua 24:15 says it like this; "As for me and my household, we will serve the Lord". Even though my sanctified mom's name is Josephine, you would have sworn that it was Joshua. We did just like he did and served the Lord. At the time, I thought she was the meanest mother in the world, but years later I realized she was only trying to save my life. Like other children at times, the things that I was told I should not do were the things I wanted to do. For years, none of us girls could wear pants. We could not attend any birthday parties that had secular music, which meant no parties, because they surely would not going to be playing church music. We could not date, and make-up was definitely out of the question. I got pissed off when other children of sanctified parents came to school bragging about a party or event they attended that played the same secular music we were supposed to run away from. I felt like this was so hypocritical, and it triggered the beginning of my rebellious years as a teenager. Me acting out caused my parents to loosen the horse collar just a little bit, but just enough for me to end up pregnant at age seventeen. It was at that point when I realized why our rules were so strict, and I regretted the day my parents compromised them. Needless to say, this is what caused me to quickly transition from girl to woman.

After finding out I was pregnant, the words of my mother began to resonate in my spirit repeatedly: "Stay a child as long as you can, because when you become an adult, there is no turning back!". As smart as I was with books, I never really understood what my mother was saying until then. It was like I had an epiphany. Somebody turned on the lights. You know the saying: "Plenty of book sense, but no street sense"; yes, unfortunately, that was me.

My days as a child were over. I am now a woman. It was not just because I had been touched sexually, but it was because of the consequences that came with my rebellious act. I had years of good upbringing, teaching, and wisdom instilled in my parents from the time I was a little girl. The good news, even in my rebellion, was that everything my parents taught me was about to be activated in my life. We were taught how to have a relationship with the Lord for ourselves. We were taught how to be independent, responsible, loving, and caring. We were taught to get as much education and knowledge as we could get our hands on because it would truly play a significant role in how well we lived our lives.

Back in the early eighties, getting pregnant as a teenager was almost taboo. It was frowned upon by the church and by society as well. My pregnancy was a devastating blow to me. I expected to be ostracized, criticized, and talked about by the world, but I did not expect that from the saints. Church was the one place I expected to embrace me, regardless of what I brought upon myself. I did not expect them to treat me like I had cooties or something. Giving birth to my daughter no doubt changed my life indefinitely. Not only did it change my life, but it saved my life. It was a wakeup call that I could no longer ignore. I was headed down the wrong road. I married my high school sweetheart, but unfortunately, he became very abusive to me in every way that you could possibly imagine. From physical, to verbal, to emotional, and spiritual, the abuse almost cost me my life. Those were some very traumatizing years for me. I cannot get that lost time back, yet I thank God. Those years helped me grow and catapulted me into the woman that I am today.

By the time I was twenty-two, I was now a mother of two children, married to a drug dealing demon, living in constant fear, and catching all kinds of hell. At one point during this time, I had to take my children with me into hiding because of a drug deal gone bad. Mind you that I never even touched the stuff. In hindsight, I wish had the courage to tell about what went on in my home, but like so many other scared young women, my loyalty was to my man. Then one day, after years of praying to God and asking him to get me out of my marriage, after being broken in every area I could be broken in, after vowing to the

Lord that I would serve him only if he got me out, he got me out! Strength, hope, and courage came out from nowhere, and I was able to step out on faith. Even though I was scared, I called around for a lawyer who would take my case with no money. That is what being a woman is all about! With all that was going on in my life, I still heard my mother's voice in my ear: "Make sure you get to know God for yourself, and make sure you always pray." I must admit that there were so many days that I wondered and wondered: "Where is God? Does he hear me? Does he see me? Does he love me like I always heard he did? And if he does, why am I going through all this hell? Why did he allow me to go down this road? Why won't he make it stop?" Yes, I blamed God for a minute, but at the same time, I knew God's intentions for my life were better than where I was in my life. It was not God's doing; it was my own, but he could surely use it and get the glory from it. After taking ownership of my mistakes and holding myself accountable, I found myself praying on a continual basis, just like I saw my mother do. In the car, at the grocery store, at the beauty salon, at the park, or wherever I was, I prayed. It was not long before I realized that turned into my mother! That was not what I wanted to do. I still wanted to go out, hang with my friends (at least the ones who stuck around after I got pregnant), smoke a cigarette, and more than anything, go to parties. Instead, I found myself praying and going to church every week. I was even going to revivals. Can you believe that? I did not realize I was being drawn into the kingdom. My life took another turn, but this time, Jesus was behind the wheel. I was trying to get it in because what I did not realize before marrying my children's father was that he was an atheist. He did not want me praying around him.

Many women will not admit to what I am about to say because of shame and out of fear of looking stupid. So, I will save them the humiliation and look stupid for them as long as other women can relate to my story. My husband was not only abusive, but he would not work. When he did get a job, he only kept it for a couple months. It was just enough to shut me up for a little while –and I do mean a little while. I thank God that for everything that I lost, I did not lose my voice. As a child, I got in trouble more than the other children and got whippings to show for it. Yes, my parents believed in them (more so my mom than my dad). Just like children do, I asked "What did I do?", and mom said, "It's that mouth of yours!" Well, this mouth of mine saved my life and is now preaching the gospel of the Lord. All praise be to God! So back to what I was saying. It is fair to say that my husband was pimping me out. He would not work half the time. I was pretty much the breadwinner. I handled all the bills and took care of our children while he ran the streets, sold drugs, and fed his appetite for other women. Once again, I heard my mother's words to us (but especially to my brothers) that if a man does not work, he does not eat. When she told us at that time, I did not know it was from the Bible. What I did know is that I wanted to eat. When I told those same words to my husband, they created an atmosphere of conflict. Before long, I just learned not to say anything to him and told everything to God. For what I was going through, I never saw anything even remotely close to this under my Mom's lock and key. I wanted out! By now, I was twenty-three years old and knew without a shadow of doubt that I did not want my children growing up in this hostile environment. Being a woman does not mean that you do not need help. I needed help, so I want back to Momma and Daddy's house.

For years, my pride and embarrassment kept me from going back home to my parents' house. I endured years of hell and abuse that I would not have had to go through...if I had just said something. In addition to that, I knew the kind of mom that I had. If she had known what my husband did to me, she would have killed him! Literally! And I did not want my mother to be locked up because of me. Years of mental, verbal, and physical abuse caused the spirit of fear to grip me like that of non-other. That became my new "normal". I knew what my husband was capable of and I did not want to jeopardize my children's safety. Either I did what he said, or he threatened to hurt my children. I felt like I needed to prove to my parents that I could stand on my own, but not like that. It was after I became free from that yoke of bondage that I realized how they only wanted the best for me. I no longer struggle with embarrassment. I have no problem speaking up and speaking out anymore. I am more transparent than glass, and I definitely do not operate under the spirit of pride anymore.

Let us fast forward. Several years passed, and I finally had the courage and strength to get out of a marriage that should have never taken place. That toxic marriage made me realize that I was not growing up, but that I had grown up. Was it easy? Absolutely not! But could it be done? Absolutely yes...because I did it. Being a woman will make you realize that getting pregnant does not always mean getting married. It means doing things the right way and waiting for marriage. Becoming a woman is one of the hardest transitions ever, especially if it is done prematurely, but with the proper upbringing, support, and a relationship with God, it can be done. How do I know? Philippians 4:13 says that I can do all things through Christ that strengthens me, and oh my God, did he strengthen me! What once seemed like an extremely hard and strict mom, is now being defined as pure love. Her countless sacrifices helped me to be the firm, mature, successful, honest, wise, and God-fearing woman that I am today.

I am still a work in progress, but it has always been my desire to pass down the morals and ethics to my children that my parents instilled in me. I am so glad that God saw the best in me, even though everyone else would only see the worst in me. Womanhood is more extensive than just age. It is about things you encounter, learn from, and can share with others to help them succeed and make it through. To God be all the glory for what he has done for me.

Senior Pastor Dr. Von Brand.

CHAPTER 6

Multidimensional Woman

SHERRELL D. MIMS

When Dr. Tenaria asked me about what it is like being a woman, the first thing that came to my mind is "multidimensional". As a woman, there are so many facets to me. One word could never describe the many hats that a woman wears. Without women in our lives, the world would not be the same. I love being a woman! In my opinion, beside Jesus, there is no greater person to be. Subjectively, I am a woman because this is the way I was born. But one of my attributes is in being a faith-filled woman of Christ. A woman like this has integrity. She is compassionate, confident, admirable, and does everything to the glory of God. She loves, lifts, and leads. As a woman of faith, I trust in the LORD and stand on his promises. And every promise God made to us is "yes" and "amen". A woman of faith keeps studying the word of God. She keeps herself refreshed in the word and maintains her faith through her prayer life.

By being a mother, a woman has the essence of God! She is the ultimate nurturer here on earth. A mother can be a mother not only to her natural children but may also bear relationships with children who are not their own (foster care and adoption). When I became a mother to my beautiful daughter Sherdell, it was an absolutely joyful experience! It did not actually feel that way when I had the labor pains, but to know I have given birth to another human being is phenomenal. At the time,

I was totally unprepared to take care of a child. As life went on, things got much better with her dad and both sides of the family assisting us.

Our daughter was a born a preemie, weighing one pound and sixteen ounces. "Wow!" is right, and it is exactly what I said when the nurses took her to the Neonatal Intensive Care Unit (NICU). Her dad followed the nurses and watched through the window as they sustained our daughter's life. I will tell anyone today; My daughter was meant to be here for such a time as this. She is a sheer joy to be around. Being a mother to my daughter meant everything to me. Although her father was there, it is a mother's unconditional love for their child(ren) that keeps a mother going. That is how I kept going... Unfortunately, her father and I divorced when she was a young age. Now, here I am, raising my daughter the best way I know how. I build up her self-esteem, supporting all her dreams, and showing her that mother's unconditional love. Let me define this in my own words: unconditional love is doing everything in your power to assist another person –with no strings attached (the operative words). When I do something for my daughter, or anyone else for that matter, I do it from the heart with integrity, and without expectation. God made me this way. He put it in my DNA! As God is a free giver, so am I.

Being a nurturer is everything to me. Mothers are born nurturers, while fathers are fixers. For me, as a nurturer, it was periods of seedtime and harvest. As I was nurturing my growing daughter, I sowed seeds of love, joy, peace, patience, and celebration. Over time, I saw her blossom into the young adult woman that she is now. Received nurturing by me, but not just me. She received it from God, and from both sides of the family (especially from the women). As of today, my daughter is currently attending one of the historically black colleges and universities (HBCU) with a major in journalism. She is part of the Golden Key Honor Society and has taken various leadership roles with campus organizations. From the seeds sown into her, they are being harvested very well.

Love. What does love have to do with it? Everything! I can literally talk about this attribute all day long, but I will keep it short and sweet. What is love? This simple question has a multitude of answers. Let me share my meaning of a woman's love. Ah, it makes the world go round. A mother's love for her child(ren) can never be wrong. There's no love like a mother-daughter bond, and I can totally relate to this in Isaiah 66:13: "As one whom his mother comforts, so I will comfort you.", and in Isaiah 49:15: "Can a mother forget her nursing child? Can she feel no love for the child she has borne?" I raised my daughter with unconditional love. A mother's love is endless, never changing, and always nurturing. The legacy of a mother's love survives, even when their days on earth are past. I thank God for being a mother. I especially thank God for mothers around the world.

I am a sister. With two brothers and four sisters in the same house, things were challenging. I am the middle child of seven siblings. Our parents raised us the best way they knew how under all circumstances. My sisters and I were very close while we grew up, and we are still close today. Let alone having sisters, having just one sister is a wonderful thing. I always had someone to play with, to argue with, and sometimes to fight with (LOL). While we grew up, we talked about our issues as women. Being a woman in today's society is a challenge in itself, but being a black woman is a totally different story. As black women growing up in a rural neighborhood, we had some tough times. I decided to break that generational cycle of being on welfare and having a poverty-stricken mentality. I decided to go to college to become a registered nurse, and I have succeeded. I was the first in my family to go to college. So, twenty years later, I stand as a strong black woman despite the odds. From one sister to another, you can do and be whatever you put your mind to do, but with Jesus at the center of it all. DREAM IT, DO IT!

Merriam-Webster defines leadership as "the power or ability to lead other people". A secondary definition that caught my eye was "capacity to lead". I have the ability to govern myself and influence others around me. I know how to showcase expected behaviors and leverage strengths so everyone in the room feels valued and appreciated. Both definitions define me as a woman with leadership skills. I can truly say that as a registered nurse (professional), I have many opportunities to lead. I am also a spiritual leader/mentor to newcomers in the church. As a woman, God uses me on many different levels to advance his kingdom.

Webster's Dictionary defines grace as "the exercise of love, kindness, favor, dispositions to benefit or serve another; favor bestowed or privilege conferred". As a woman of grace, this is easy for me to perform. I always think about grace in the sense that I received it. If it was not for God's grace and mercy, where would I be? I have an attitude of gratitude toward my LORD and Savior because of what he did on the cross for an undeserving wretch like me. I AM GRACE!

---

25 Strength and honor are her clothing, and she
shall rejoice in time to come. 26 She openeth her
mouth with wisdom; in her tongue is the law of
kindness. 27 She looketh well to the ways of her
household, and eateth not the bread of idleness.
28 Her children arise up, and call her blessed; her
husband also, and he praiseth her. 29 Many
daughters have done virtuously, but thou excellest
them all. 30 Favour is deceitful, and beauty is vain:
but a woman that feareth the Lord, she shall be
praised. 31 Give her of the fruit of her hands; let her
own works praise her in the gates.

Proverbs 31:25-31

These are the scriptures that describe me. I am that modern day Proverbs 31 woman.

CHAPTER 7

The Delicate Vessel

VALJON M. LYONS

I had to ponder that question for a minute or so. Then I asked myself again: what is it like being a woman? To me, being a woman means being strong and being the weaker or delicate vessel at the same time (1 Peter 3:7; Proverbs 31:10). Being a woman means being a virtuous and powerful woman who knows my value. I know my worth is far more than rubies, and I expect to be respected accordingly. Women have different shapes, sizes, and colors. We come from different backgrounds and ethnic groups. We are all women, but what separates me from being just another woman is that I have decided to follow God (Yahweh). As a woman of God, I am differentiated from the world because I have decided to follow the Creator himself. This does not make me better, but it makes me different. It does not mean that I am exempt from the cares of life, but the difference is seen as I go through personal trials and tribulations. I look to God for direction and for comfort. He is my sole provider. As a woman of God, I take the time to ask God for his help, wisdom, guidance, counsel, and strength. The LORD is my shepherd (Psalm 23). He is Jehovah-Jireh, and I have no lack!

What is it like being a woman? It means me being a woman who does not walk in condemnation but who now walks in grace. I am in Christ, therefore there is no condemnation (Romans 8:1). I am a woman who embraces my imperfections, knowing that I am imperfectly perfect. I have grace, but not because of anything that I have done, but only because it is grace that comes from God. As a woman of God, I am able to use oppositions as opportunities, recognizing how that problem that I might face has purpose. I am fully persuaded that God's promises are sure ("...though it tarry, wait for it;" - Habakkuk 2:3 KJV).

Even through tears, sleepless nights, long days, heartache and pain, we know we must preserve ourselves. Being a woman of God allows me to stand strong during trying and uncertain times. It is God who keeps me. Keep in mind: this is not the same woman that the world knows because that woman tends to throw in the towel, wave the white flag of surrender, run to the world for counsel, or run to a man for the solution. I stand strong because I am not standing in my own strength (2 Chronicles 20:17) Because I was weak, I can now say that I am strong through God (Joel 3:10).

As a woman of God, I understand that I must pray and seek God daily because it is HE who gives me strength. I would rather be different. I would rather be the one that has courage like Esther, doing things that are unprecedented. She went before the king unannounced and wound up saving an entire nation (Esther 5:1-8). I would rather have an anointing like Deborah the prophetess (Judges 4:4), or the tenacity and love of Ruth, who stayed with Naomi after all her sons died during a famine in the land (Ruth 1:1). I can always go to the word of God for guidance, correction, support, strength, healing, and instruction. I can go to God for anything because he loves me just that much. I may go boldly before the throne of grace to obtain mercy and find grace in time of need (Hebrews 4:16). Thank God for his Son Jesus, who allows me to have that access.

Before I go to anyone, he is the first One I go to. The beauty of this is that in his word, I can see how his follower's handled life. The word of God says it was written for my learning (Romans 15:4). I can also see how imperfect women like me can make positive marks in the world that cannot be erased. Rahab was a harlot (Judges 2:1-3; 6:17), but her faith placed her into the lineage of Christ (Matthew 1:5)!

As a woman from New Orleans who comes from a large family. I learned how to be a woman of God from my mother, Beverly Nelson Marcelin, who taught us the word of God. Every morning before we left the house, she would anoint me and my siblings with holy oil. Sometimes while we slept, we heard her come into the bedroom, praying and anointing our heads with oil. When I became a teenager, I started asking her to anoint my hands because I did not want to go to school with so much oil running down my forehead. I began to realize why my skin was so oily! But what was instilled in me stayed with me, so as I got older, I mimicked what I saw my mother do. I am the mother of one amazing and beautiful daughter, Kristian Ann Lyons. This is why I taught her to serve God –and to serve God only. Because I was born to lead, I knew that I had to lead by example. Now this is not to say that I am perfect or never made any mistakes—because I made many mistakes—but I learned and grew from them. I know that God loves me, despite all my mistakes. To lead by example, I knew that this life is something I could not do on my own. I had to turn to the One who created all things. I had to turn to the One who created me (John 1:1)!

I love being a woman and being connected to God. Although the man carries life, it is the woman who incubates and nourishes life. God is amazing! I know my role as a woman, and it is what makes me a phenomenal woman of God. Someone asked me what I meant by playing my "role". I explained that I know and accept my place in the body of Christ. It is HE who made me his daughter, and a help meet to his son. I am not just a woman. I am a woman of God, and a daughter of the Most High. You cannot come any better than that, right? So, if someone asks me about my womanhood, I can easily and proudly answer that I am a woman of God first. I do not let my struggles, my past, and the opinions of others define me. No matter what I do, I will always have naysayers, but let them say on. What they say does not matter anyway. Praise God!

Additional reference scriptures: Proverbs 22:6; John 16:33; 2 Corinthians 6:18

CHAPTER 8

The Gift

CURLYN DALEY

As a growing child, no one tells you how your life will plan out. During my school years, my mother often sounded like a broken record: "Put yuh head to yuh book!". She believed that education would set us up for life. If my teachers could see me now, they would not believe I am the same child that often got into trouble. I hung out with the wrong people. I was that prankster, that bully, that truant who had frequent trips to the headmasters' office. My teachers often reminded me that there was no hope for me if my behavior did not improve. When I left school, I took some qualifications with me (nothing to shout home about), but I had no behavior change. But I did not allow my childhood to shape my future.

I was one of seven children. My two eldest brothers did not live at home. They were married and had their own families, but they still visited every week for Sunday dinner. It was something we always looked forward to. During Sunday mealtimes, there were two things my parents always discussed. They are things that never departed from our memories. One of those things was about going back home to Jamaica, where they were building a house. That other thing was about God coming back soon. I grew up in the city of Stoke-on-Trent (in Staffordshire, England). Because Stoke was predominantly white, I had a lot of Caucasian friends. The black people who lived in Stoke-on-Trent all knew each other, but the only time I saw most of them was when there was a church convention. When I dated my boyfriend, I would sneak and visit him in Wolverhampton on Saturdays. In comparison to Stoke, Wolverhampton was a diverse city, so I was excited that there was a community of black Afro-Caribbean people. At this time in my life, it was the only time I saw so many black people living in one area. My mother woke up one morning and instructed me to visit the doctors. I followed through and to my surprise, it was confirmed that I was pregnant indeed. She dreamed right. I must admit how after my first sexual encounter, I knew in my mind and my body that I was pregnant. I felt warm and funny inside, so after my mother's premonition and instruction, there was no surprise. As many Jamaican children can vouch, when our mothers dream, they dream correctly. It is something I cannot explain –but it happens.

My mother always threateningly said to us young girls that if we came home pregnant, we had to leave home. The ten-minute journey between home and the doctor's office felt like an hour. It was filled with tears, disappointment, and fear of having to confirm to my parents that I was pregnant. And then there were the repercussions. What did I know about motherhood at eighteen years of age? Still unsure of what I was going to do or where I would go, I kept in mind what my mother always said so. When I got home, I started packing my bags. My heartbeat was faster when I heard my mother's footsteps approaching my bedroom door. She asked me about what the doctor said, and with tears rolling down my face, I told her how the doctor confirmed I was pregnant. She started shouting at me, but to my surprise, she was referring to why I had my bags packed! She told me I was not going anywhere, but...I did have to tell my father. Even though I felt relief from the first part of what she said, I felt a tense panic from the second part. How was I going to tell my father that his little girl was now with child? I thought "No way!", my mum would have to tell him. Throughout my pregnancy, my father, an incredibly quiet and reserved man, never once asked me anything about it. We lived next door to a chip shop, and they sold steak and kidney pies that I loved. Dad's way of making sure I was alright was by asking if I wanted a pie.

With mixed feelings of joy and sadness because of my unplanned pregnancy at age eighteen, I gave birth to my son Trevor in January 1983. He was a beautiful seven-pound two ounce bouncing baby. My baby. He had the resemblance of my father. I left my parent's home in June 1983 and moved in with my son's father Craig, his mother, and his other siblings. We decided to move in with them because my parents and younger siblings were due to migrate to Jamaica. By this time, their house construction was done, and it was ready for them to move into. My mother wanted me and Trevor to move with them, but I thought I was now a grown woman with a man, our baby, and a new life. In August 1983, Craig's mother died. Her funeral was a small occasion, and a small reception was kept at the home. It was on this occasion that Craig hit me in front of everyone. He thought I had not given him as large a portion of food as his brothers, so he slapped me so hard that the plate fell out of my hand. This was the first time he hit me, but little did I know that it would not be the last time. I immediately grabbed our son and ran upstairs. I was so embarrassed. I excused his behavior, believing that he was grieving over his mother's death. This was the first time I encountered domestic violence, but I did not recognize it as such. It was not long after this that my father passed. My younger siblings were at home, but Craig would not allow me to go there until the weekend. He said it was because he had to work, and he did not want me travelling on my own. I was heartbroken. My mother promised Dad that she would still migrate to Jamaica with my siblings, and by December 1983, they were there.

I suffered abuse over a period of four years before leaving Craig. I left our son with Craig because by this time, I was not able to care for him or myself. I moved into a women's hostel because for all the times I went to go stay with a girlfriend, Craig found out where I was and kicked her door off to get in. To save her from any further trouble, I would just leave with him. He made it hard for me to spend time with any of my friends. He found chores for me to do before allowing me to go out, and if I came back home late, he beat me. On one occasion, I came home to him waiting for me with a baseball bat. According to him, I came back too late. The next day, I was bruised all over and unable to pick my son up. I was on eggshells, not wanting to upset Craig, but he acted as though nothing happened. He forced me to have sex and if I did not want to, he put me in a tub of cold water and beat me in the bath. Afterward, he made me to sleep on the floor (sometimes until morning) or in our son's room.

With feelings of loss, emptiness and loneliness, I felt I had nowhere to turn. There was no other solution for me than to be gone from existence. I had enough. I twice attempted to commit suicide by overdosing on paracetamol tablets, but Craig came home and called the ambulance after realizing what I did. It was that second time where, although I wanted to die, a part of me wanted to live, but I was so low and could see no way out. Waking up the next morning confirmed that I was once again unsuccessful. I made a conscious decision to find an alternative way to escape, so instead of going home, I referred myself into a woman's hostel. What I thought I escaped came after me with a vengeance. He found us. The torment resumed when I said "no" to his proposals to get back together. He beat me until I was unconscious. I woke up in a hospital room, wondering where my son was and if he was ok. I opened my eyes to Craig leaning over me, asking me if I was alright while he stroked my face. To him, it was as if someone else had done this to me. Was this a dream or a joke? My friend Stephanie was with me. Wanting me to press charges, she called the hospital staff, and they called the police. Pressing charges was a distant thought in my mind. I feared the repercussions, but after sound advice and persuasion, I followed through. I had broken ribs, blackened eyes, and my face was disfigured and unrecognizable. I was in the hospital for about two weeks before being discharged. As for Craig, all he received from court proceedings was one-hundred twenty-five hours of community service and a one-hundred pound fine. Even though the court placed an injunction for him not to come near me, he continued to taunt me. He did this even after he began a new relationship with someone else. Months went by before he eventually left me completely alone.

I became very promiscuous after leaving that relationship, believing I was not worthy of being loved and feeling ashamed of how I allowed the abuse to happen. Craig stripped me of my identity, so I lacked confidence. I just did not care anymore. I became hard and desensitized so I would not get hurt again. To prevent the hurt, I dated different men who had their own partners. It took a long period of time for me to begin to trust again. After some years, I met Ronnie, the man who would become my first husband. He was a man who had his own partner, but I still engaged him in a sexual relationship. There is a saying that "what goes around, comes around", and I am a great believer in this. Even though I knew he had a partner, I did not let that stop me. I just wanted to protect myself. As time went on, Ronnie left his partner as our feelings for each other grew. Soon after, I gave birth to our daughter Chedene in March 1993 after a difficult pregnancy. I miscarried once before, but to God be the glory, she arrived. This was a joyous occasion in my life. Things were going well between me and Ronnie, so we discussed getting married and purchasing our own property. Never mind that by now, there were so many red flags and signs screaming out at me, "What are you doing?!" He was involved in several affairs during our relationship and, three children later, that still did not faze me. I loved him. As women, we sometimes believe that we can change a man. This was not the case. We got married in July 1998. It was a big wedding, a grand affair, the talk of the town. By now, we had already moved into our new home in Wolverhampton, where Ronnie was well known. Being with him made me feel great. Most people thought we would never marry, but we had them fooled. Or should I say how I fooled myself! He was my heartbeat. I was so in love with him because he gave me a sense of security I never had before. In 2000, we separated because this time I was the one who had an affair (plot twist, I know). After many times of trying to get back together, we amicably decided to call it a day and ended our marriage. We remain good friends.

After sharing your life with someone, the process of divorce is so heart-rending and final. Although I vowed never to marry again, I remarried in 2013, but with a deep foundation in Christian values. I knew it was not right for me to live in fornication. My amazing husband Alton was from Jamaica, but he did not have immigration status. After we got married, we made several attempts to resolve this issue. In October 2017, he was advised to return to Jamaica and resume his application from there. By that time, I had been serving God for thirteen years, but after meeting with a Christian friend, she encouraged me to change the direction of my Christian walk. I knew I did not want to go back into the world, but after more reflection, I made up my mind that I was going to surrender all to Christ. It was as though God catapulted my life from that moment: "And I will restore to you the years that the locust has eaten" (Joel 2:25) Although Alton and I were apart, this was a season of self-discovery. My relationship with God grew stronger, and I began to walk into my purpose. I had faith and trusted God to return my husband to me. In January 2020, Alton was approved to return!

Although my journey has been hard, I thank God that my life never ended. If the enemy succeeded, I would not be here today to see my life transitioned. I would not have been able to know that the power of God to endure those things I went through is a GIFT: "Every good gift and every perfect gift is from above" (James 1:17). Teenage pregnancy, domestic violence, bereavement, adultery, divorce, sickness, and a failed marriage are the life experiences that I use to empower other women. I continue to shape and develop my life to do what God has called me to do. These experiences have given me a clearer awareness of my true identity in Christ. They have made me brave, bold, strong, and have given me a can-do ideology. With every challenge I face, I know that I am able to face it head on, enabling me to continue growing as the confident and independent God-fearing woman I have become today.

CHAPTER 9

The It Factor

DR. CAROLYN P. MOWBRAY

I vividly remember observing two generations of matriarchs adorning glamorous outfits on many occasions. From foundation garments and nylon stockings to the layering of lotion and perfume. The ensemble was complete with lipstick, earrings, pearls, stilettos, and furs, when appropriate. These garments represented socio-economic status in my community. As I grew-up, I realized the clothes, though beautiful, did not make these women. My mother and paternal grandmother were clothed in faith, strength, confidence, and inner beauty. Their presence made an impact and transformed atmospheres. These experiences were my early exposure that began my journey. As a child, I could not articulate "what they had" but I wanted "it!" The "IT" factor began my quest. At four years old, I began collecting visual images and forming mental lists of what I thought I liked. I started with my love for pearls, stilettos and lipstick. I was determined to be clothed in the same confidence, boldness and walk in faith with what I witnessed daily. I did not understand how my role models earned their right to speak with authority as women of excellence. I was the gracious recipient of the finished product. I did not know their history and all the time it took. I was too young to even understand the cost of "IT"...being a woman. Their work, blood, sweat, tears, loss and joys of life's journey afforded them that esteemed honor. Upon leaving the security of my parent’s home at age six, my process and my story began. I would soon understand what it meant to be a woman.

A woman is defined in the Merriam Webster's Dictionary as " a female person, a help mate, help meet, a lady, Madam, Missus, old lady, wife, wifey,". Whatever the definition, a woman is created and built by her life experiences. That is a fact. My first acquaintance with these creative markers began in elementary school. Immediately, I was familiar with rejection because I struggled with obesity. Growing up in the late nineteen-sixties, bullying was not considered abusive., but it caused emotional disruption in my life. I was taught to handle ridicule and name calling ("Sticks and stones may break my bones but words will never hurt me"). I was told to "suck it up" because there will be numerous distractions like that for the rest of my life. I was not a confrontational person, so that is exactly what I did. I ignored the bullies, and the distraction piled on. At home, I secretly cried in my room after school. My parents did not know how deeply I was affected. Many years later, I continued feeling rejected and insignificant. I was emotionally withdrawn until I realized I had something to offer. I had the ability to make friends easily. I discovered people actually liked me. But these people did not look like me. They were not from my community or culture. I assimilated to their different culture. It became easy for me. I adopted their way of speaking and their look. I became a social chameleon. I found safety and a comfort zone. I had new friends who were attracted to my intellect and my style.

I became an influencer and gatherer of people. I had a busy social calendar. Little did I know that my ability to become a chameleon would follow me throughout my life.

I did not choose to go to an HBCU (historically black college and university), as my parents preferred. I extended myself far beyond the borders of where I lived. I learned to cross barriers that some people thought were embarrassing. Being able to go beyond personal borders allowed miracles to happen. I found favor. I made friends who had access and opportunities for me as a young woman. In academia, I had an eye-opening experience, but not the eye-opening experience I expected. I was stereotyped as the underachiever. College was supposed to be a challenge for me, and a defeat as well. But I was not defeated. I was victorious in every challenge.

In my early years as a wife and mother, I blossomed and had amazing growth as a young adult. Leaving my parents' home and starting my own household with my husband was a good thing. I was the family manager. Life was a beautiful experience. I wanted to be married, and I wanted to be a mother. Simultaneously, I was finished my academic career. As a new registered nurse, I embarked on a new journey of challenges. I still examined what it was that I liked about being a woman. Finding myself, defending my womanhood, and being a woman of color came together in many situations and all of them with different obstacles. As a young adult, being a woman was a huge responsibility. I embraced it. I enjoyed it. I loved being a mother and a wife. I took pride in my home, as I saw my mother and grandmother do. I was the manager, housekeeper, and cook. I learned early that being a woman is about taking hold, embracing, and changing. Two people coming together as one is difficult, but I did not give up. I was headstrong. I wanted to persevere in my vows so the marriage covenant would be successful. I wanted to accomplish it all. I wanted to do what I saw each woman do before me. I found out how that was not my destiny. That was not what was going to happen for me.

Being a young black American registered nurse, I had barriers orchestrated by nurses of privilege. My appearance automatically sets me up as the underdog. During my new graduate orientation, nursing staff said and did things that were demonstrative. In my presence, certain things were stated, like "she's slower than...". But I could not have cared less. I remained focused as I was invested in my career. I knew it was my chosen profession. I endured many hardships and rose above people who anticipated my failure. In time, I became extremely successful. I did not fear the testing because I had tools, knowledge, and understanding. I was never overwhelmed or dissatisfied. Thirty-five years later, I still have career satisfaction. I enjoy being a bedside clinician. It is a commitment of intellect, physical, and spiritual being. I like being a woman who is a nurse. It is what and where I am called to be.

Motherhood comes with its own lessons. Unexpectedly, I became a single parent. I did not sign up for that. My husband, the father of my two children, decided to be a crackhead. I was ignorant to the fact that my husband had the disease of addiction. In the midst of the crack cocaine era, my husband got hooked. The disease manifested, and it took its toll on our family. I started building up walls and barriers against everything vile and volatile that came our way. The process of addiction damaged the fortress around our marriage. It traumatized our children. The domestic violence and intimate partner abuse that followed were extremely unfamiliar to me. We lost many things during that experience, but the most significant things we lost was each other. We lost the love and mutual respect for one another, but I fought to see our marriage through to the end. Every violent injury and insult, whether emotional or physical, shook the foundation of my being. It disturbed everything I believed in. I was knocked off of my pedestal. The rug was pulled out from under me. I was down on my back, but my children needed me to be present with them in the moment. I could not withdraw from life, but I wanted to disappear. I sank lower and lower into depression. I was barely functioned from day to day. I felt like I was drowning. I never spoke or expressed a word to anybody, and I never cried out for help. I never demanded to get back what was mine. I never called attention to what I was going through. I was in shock, thinking how "This cannot be my life!". My dear mother was ill and grieved the transition of my father. It was all so painful. My family was overwhelmed by death and loss. We needed help.

Being shaped and molded into a woman is not a pleasant process. I learned to take authority over destiny destroyers. I entered a season of recalibration. My life regained boundaries and stability. I resolved to forgive my ex-husband and I also managed to forgive myself. I like being a woman who has choices and options. I chose to save my family and to rise above our challenges and move forward. As a woman, I liked being a positive impact on woman. I still have many beautiful experiences that afford me points of inspiration. Being a woman is being a beautiful creature whose beauty is carved out from life's insults and injuries. What I have seen in the mirror, from childhood to a seasoned queen, is amazing. I own every stage of womanhood. I am a woman for all seasons. I value my time to rediscover my dreams and desires. I chose to rid my life of toxins; the people, places, and things that can kill, steal, and destroy me. I like being a mature grown-up and the best woman

I can be. As a woman, I appreciate the beauty that begins as the expression of the inner "me". I have been transformed through many portals, and I evolved. The negatives and the positives pressed and peeled me until the essence of my womanhood was revealed. "My people" know that I like my own, exclusive definition of being a woman. Most importantly, I am able to facilitate other women as they take their journey. My womanhood was chosen for me before I was created in my mother's womb. I am a phenom, predestined to be a woman. And I like that. I am the universal expression of femininity. There have been moments where I wanted to give up, but I could not give up. It was not an option. I have a genetic, internal drive that says, "No matter what, we keep on going". For the legacy, I keep on going. As a matriarch, I keep on going. I have assignments that are not yet finished, but I keep on going. Yes!!! Being a woman involves the hair, the nails, the stilettos, the lipstick, the pearls, and the perfume. Yes, it is all those things, but I like being a woman who has the determination, strength, courage, boldness, integrity, and character that every decade of life has built in me. The "IT" factor.

CHAPTER 10

My Fairytale

MONIQUE FRANCOIS

Me: Hi Mommy! Guess what?

Mom: What, baby girl?

Me: I know what I'll be when I grow up

Mom: You know already? At six years old?

Me: Yes! I'll be a mom. A man is coming on a white horse. He will be strong and handsome. His eyes are just for me. He will grab me, hold me tight in his arms, and I will be his wife, and he will be my husband. Forever and ever, right Mommy?

Mom: Right, baby girl.

In the church world, we have women's conferences, meetings, and other occasions where we express how the Bible defines a woman. But what does it mean to be born with the designated "female" sex on your birth certificate? I have to go back to the beginning.

Growing up in the Bronx, I was one of seven children from the union of Dorothy Avery Francois and John Lloyd Francois. Of five boys and two girls, I was the third child and first girl, with a sister born behind me. Surrounded by five brothers, I found out what it was like to be a woman, or soon to be one anyway. I was able to keep up with my brothers with running, digging in the dirt, and the rough play. I kept up with my brothers alright, but I was so glad when my mother bought me beautiful dresses and bows for my hair. Finally, I started to feel "pretty". I felt like a woman.

Then my fairytale changed. Mom told me that before I was born, Daddy said to her, "Why can't you get an abortion?". So, being the first girl, I began to feel unwanted. Maybe this "girl" thing was not so great after all. I began to see what some differences between being a girl and being a boy were. There seemed to be a double standard going on. Boys and men could come and go as they pleased, but girls and women had to be kept close by. If an unmarried woman got pregnant, it was as if the woman did it by herself.

As I got older, the fairytale was not only crushed, but it began to fade and became a once in a while daydream. The man on the white horse was not coming for me. I began to see more of a difference between the boys and me as a growing young woman. It was a dark night in the Bronx projects. Like I mentioned earlier, we were seven children in the same house, so sleeping arrangements were tight. This particular night I remember sleeping with one of my younger brothers on a bunk bed. I slept at the outside edge to prevent my younger, smaller brother from falling out. It was then that I realized that I was "different". I woke up suddenly to see a family member standing over me, with his hand where it should not be. I kept this a secret for about fifty years.

The fairytale got dimmer and dimmer. I was about twelve years old when a man followed me and my sister into an elevator. When the door closed, he proceeded to put his hand inside my sleeveless blouse. Then he exposed himself to my sister and me before running out of the elevator. That ended my fairytale of becoming a woman, and the man on the white horse was not coming for me. Maybe this was just a young girl's fairytale after all.

Soon after that incident, compounded with prior incidents, I wished that I could not be seen at all. Not by the man on the white horse, or by anyone. I began to walk with my head down. By this time, I wore glasses and braces that only helped my insecurities. Wherever I went, I just wanted to fade into the walls. The glasses and braces only made me more of a target. "Ugly", "metal mouth", "four eyes", and "Olive Oyl" were names I heard frequently. I took those words and embraced them. I wore them like a comfortable coat. I started wearing clothes that I thought would cover me up. The fairytale had long vanished by this time.

I stayed in this wallflower mode for a while. I became a selective mute, speaking only at home but never speaking at school unless I had to. If I was asked a question, I mumbled inaudibly. Although I was in the top classes, the teachers sent me to speech classes, etc. I continued into junior high school in this introverted state. My grades were high, but so was my introversion.

Because my grades were high, I got a scholarship to a private high school in Ohio. I would be an exchange student living with a family. This family was saved, as God orchestrated it. I continued being the "odd" one, and that helped to push me further into my studies. I graduated from a prominent private high school in Ohio, with only two blacks in my graduating class.

Ohio was totally different from the Bronx. I grew up in a project building, but now I lived in a house. It was a wonderful experience. It started to find some of "me" inside me. I was getting a different view of life, but I was still in a prison inside of my own mind.

Moving right along from junior high school through high school, I graduated. I was then back in the Bronx and about to attend college. I decided to become a nurse. I wanted to see people be healed and happy. I still classified myself as an introvert and a self-proclaimed loner. It made me feel better to think that me being a loner was self-proclaimed, and not because I felt like I was unwanted.

Into my second year of clinical training, I was introduced to an engineering student. This man was not on a white horse; in fact, he could barely speak English! But he gave me the time of day, and he seemed interested in me. My fairytale faded long ago, so I tried to piece it back together in my mind. Maybe it was not a white horse. Was it a foreign student who came on a plane? Was the man on the horse supposed to be tall or short? Was he to speak to me in another language? Were we supposed to go off into the sunset on a horse or in a plane? Or on the subway? Well, maybe it was just a fantasy of what it would be like to be a happy woman.

Soon after I graduated, I got married. I was never asked to marry before, so I thought it might be my only chance. Besides, I thought, who else would really want me? In my mind, I was still wearing that "ugly" coat that I was so comfortable in. The engineering student was still finishing up his degree, but in the meantime...I gave birth to five children. I was able to bear children, and after all, the minister said, "I now pronounce you man and wife...". I was a woman now! Yeah!

My revised fairytale started to slowly fade away. The honeymoon phase quickly dissolved. I began working, the children started coming, but my husband was still in school. I worked as a registered nurse through five pregnancies. Then, manipulation, control, and emotional abuse began. So, I thought, this "woman" thing is not like what I heard it would be like. My dream of a strong man holding me close to protect me passed me by, but I held onto the idea that I had to be "strong". So many things happened to me before, so by that time, it was just another thing for me to overcome. I kept a smile on my face and went to work, taking care of people who could not take care of themselves. But as I went home each day, I became despondent. What about me? Was I forgotten?

One day, I started holding my head up instead of looking down. I remembered the Bible stories my mom used to tell me. I remembered the Sunday school lessons she taught me, and lined them up with the Word that I began to read. I finally saw what the Bible said about being a woman, and not just about being female. I prayed, and was led to a church home. I repented for my sins and realized that Jesus suffered for me, just to redeem ME! the woman he made me to be! My little girl's dream came back to me! The man on the white horse was Jesus Christ coming for me, and yes, He has His eye on me! Yes, He will hold me with His strong arm, I will be His bride and He will be the Husbandman. "Thou hast loved righteousness, and hated iniquity; therefore God, even thy God hast anointed thee with the oil of gladness above thy fellows." (Hebrews 1:9 KJV) I eventually needed this scripture as part of my daily life.

Soon after I received Jesus in my life, I realized the power in me becoming a praying woman! I was told by the enemy, "You are stronger than I thought you were." I said yes, I am stronger than even "I" thought I was. The enemy was not happy. I was given the ultimatum not to go back to my church, but for me, it was not the church; it was the relationship with the God of the church. I found that man and protector I dreamt of so many years ago. "My beloved is mine, and I am his...." (Song of Solomon 2:16 KJV). I was not willing to let go of my God, and because of this reality, I eventually got divorced.

I have been on my own for over twenty years now. I have been holding on to the right hand of my Savior. Now I am ready to be made whole. To dream again. To live again. Not to just be female, but to be that submissive woman who is strong in faith. To be the woman God called me to be. I, with the help of God, HAD to hold it together spiritually and naturally as a single mother now of five. I recently overcame a near-fatal experience, and more than ever, I realize I have purpose in the Lord. My childhood fairytale is now a spiritual reality. The difference in becoming a strong woman or staying a defeated woman came through a spiritual battle. Now, my latter days will be my better days. My dream is coming to fruition, spiritually and naturally, in Jesus' name. Amen. My worship is for real!

CHAPTER 11

Servanthood

DR. KIM BEST

I am Kim Best, aka Dr. Kim Best, the eldest of five siblings. I was born, raised, and attended school in Brooklyn, New York. I am the glue that holds the family together. I began my servant journey by working in the community at age twelve, where my first employment was with the Bedford Stuyvesant Restoration Corporation. In their community center. I was able to help provide various resources and partnerships. At age nineteen, I joined my first political organization. It was there that I had the pleasure of meeting and working with the late congresswoman Shirley Chisholm. She was very instrumental toward my growth as a young woman, and as a mentor in the community. I furthered my community service and met other influential women who exposed me to other opportunities and leadership positions.

Because of my interest in the community, I joined a number of organizations and began my community service career. Today, I am president of a local precinct community council, chairman of an advisory board, a community board member, and member of a few civic organizations. I have special memories of my late parents, mother Martha Best and father Albert Best, who supported me in all my endeavors. Losing my father in 2020 to COVID-19 was a challenge. It was a new beginning in my life and, with a few adjustments, it led to my retirement from thirty-two years of municipal public service. God closed one door and opened another in my spiritual life by elevating me to Regional Apostle and Chief Apostle in the ministry. I asked for his grace and mercy in allowing me to continue serving him and building up his kingdom. I am able to flourish as a woman, no matter what I do, because I am able to serve.

CHAPTER 12

Getting Back Up Again

JEAN THOMPSON

Being a woman is not easy, but it is very much rewarding. Being a single mother of two daughters and one son, I have seen it all and have been through it all. From an early age, I was always interested in heels, purses and makeup. Girly things were always at the top of the list of things I wanted. I acquired my first genuine Coach bag at fourteen years old. My mom said I could purchase it with my first summer youth job paycheck. That was a huge deal for me. I followed in the footsteps of my two older sisters. I wanted whatever they had. They had jobs and could buy a lot of fancy things, so I wanted the same. Even at a young age, I tried doing all the things they did, like smoking cigarettes and partying. One day when I caught them smoking, I wanted to do the same, not realizing they were bad for our health. Mom was not happy with them when she found out they gave me my first cigarette. I started to enjoy it. I smoked more, and by the time I was sixteen years old, I started drinking beer.

On another day, a few of my girlfriends and I planned a Saturday night out. We went to a club where the music was so loud, we could not hear each other speak. Some guys at the club asked if we wanted to dance and have drinks. I refused. I never let guys buy my drinks at clubs. Thankfully, (and gratefully), I was cautious. When I got my drink, I drank it right where I was. My girlfriend left her drink and came back for it later, but by that time, one of the guys spiked her drink. Later that night, he tried to attack her in the ladies bathroom. From that time and on, I always warn women to never buy drinks and leave them unattended. Even though I was a young woman, I was observant and discerning about danger lurking.

I grew up a lot faster than I may have wanted to. It was not the way I wanted to. At the tender age of eight years old, I was physically and verbally assaulted by a male cousin and an uncle. The abuse went on for years because I was afraid and too embarrassed to share that horrific experience with my family. One day, I decided to inform my oldest sister about what took place throughout those years. She said I could have told her about it when it happened, and I told her about how I was too scared to do it. I did not want the family to separate or be ridiculed by our neighbors. At that time, our family had a great reputation in the community. If word got out, imagine what the talk about us would have been like in those days? Incest running rampant in my family. That would have been unheard of! The unwanted actions by those two family members taught me later in my life to be very cautious about bringing new guys around my daughters. I never allowed my daughters to spend the night out, except if they were at my mother's or sister's house. I never let men spend the night at my house. I wanted to make sure my son and daughters would always be safe in their own home. The experience of being physically and verbally abused as a young child became a mental strain that affected my life for years after. It took some time for me to begin relationships, and it was that much harder for me to trust men.

I was a guarded young woman. My heart was closed off, but the time came when I decided to begin dating and learning to trust. I was sixteen years old when I met a young man who would become the father of my first daughter. He was working in a diner where I went to have lunch after school was out. He was the manager, and he would come over to take my order where I sat at the counter. He was a mature, very good-looking, charming and charismatic guy. We exchanged phone numbers and he promised to give me a call. Before we made a date to go out, I had my family check him out. I invited my older sister to go with me to his diner, and we sat and talked for a while. She agreed that he was good looking, but noticed that he was a little older than me. She was ok with me going out to dinner with him, but she also told me to be sure not to leave my food and drink unattended.

The next weekend, I went out on a date with him to a local park during the daytime so we could walk, talk, and get to know each other. I figured late nights were too inviting and might lead to other ideas. We continued to see each other and dated for about a year. In the beginning, he was kind and caring. He bought me flowers and boxes of candy for many of our dates. He even started to splurge lots of his paychecks on me with pretty heels and purses. He knew exactly how to keep me smiling. Every week when we went out, we were dressed to the nines with our jackets and shoes in matching colors (and a new purse for me). I really fell for this guy, and he said he felt the same about me. I felt his love for me too. I thought I hit the jackpot. My friends were so happy and elated that I was the first among us to be in a great relationship. He met my Mom and siblings, as I had already met his Mom and extended family. We thought we were ready to start a family, so we decided to consummate our relationship. I had one more year left in high school, and he was working and already had his own place.

Everything was falling into place. We had enough room for a newborn, and he was saving money to get ready for parenthood. He was so overprotective of me. He never allowed me to go see friends, or be at many of our family functions. I thought that was a good thing at the time...until he became more jealous and aggressive with me. We were always around each other, and the relationship became very strained during the later months of my pregnancy. He became physically aggressive and very volatile at times. I was under the impression he was tired from the long work hours. I also thought it was about me not having food cooked by the time he got in sometimes, but I was sick and tired most times due to the pregnancy. He became absolutely controlling, domineering, and mentally intimidating. My girlfriends were not allowed to come to visit. I kept my Mom in the dark about what went on because I wanted her to think I was okay and could be on my own. After my daughter was born and I felt stronger, I knew I had to get away because I felt like a prisoner in my own home. I knew this relationship was over when he burned my leg with a hot iron. I almost killed him that night. I left him bleeding on the floor with a cut to his throat. I had to get out of that house because I was either going to die or go to jail. And what would have happened to my child? My Mom was all I could think about. She moved far away, but he did not know where she moved to. My eldest sister also lived in the same neighborhood as Mom, so they gave me shelter. I left my baby in my Mom's care while I went to work. It was not easy, but I was able to get back up again.

Worship of the Lord was instilled in me at an early age. My great-grandmother took me and my sisters to church every Sunday. Mom worked hard as a registered nurse. A lot of the weekends were filled with overtime, but she was still able to raise six children and keep a diligent schedule for us. She made sure that we read and studied the word of God. She prayed for us every morning and night, always telling us to keep God first in all situations and circumstances. I thank God for leading and guiding me in all my ways. I almost lost my life being in a dangerous and tumultuous relationship, but God saved me. I had to get free because I had a nervous breakdown during that relationship, but the Lord restored my mental capacity. He gave me the strength and courage to get back up again.

Some years later, I was able to find a beautiful apartment for me and my daughter to live in. With just the two of us, we lived, laughed, and loved together. My life flourished with beauty and luster for a few years, and then out of the blue, I met an Army soldier through a girlfriend. He was tall, dark, handsome, a terrific cook, and very good with children. He courted me like a gentleman by holding the car door open and pulling out a chair for me at restaurants and such. Then there were the roses that came for birthdays, Mother's Day and other holidays or celebrations. We spoke late nights by telephone and wrote letters to each when we were apart. My daughter loved him. He had so much patience with her and helped out with her math homework. He was a great mathematician and worked out the problems quickly with her. We stayed together for years while we discussed future plans for marriage and more children. We were married in July 1981. We had a small guest list of family and close friends. In August 1983, my second daughter was born. I never had to lift a thing doing any housework. He did it all. He never complained about it or did it grudgingly. We joined and attended church together as a family. He was raised by both his parents, and he exhibited their characteristics. In making our family his priority, he led by example. He was an amazingly sweet dad to his girls, speaking highly of them to others. He loved me and treated with the utmost respect. In 1988, our son was born. He was the child who sealed our marriage. Our relationship was full and complete.

During these early years, I was smitten by his love of family. I believed he had no wrongdoing, but I guess he began to get bored with the commitment. I became displeased at him for not coming straight home on the weekends. I had no idea about what kept him so captivated outside our home. He went out and partied more and more with his friends. He began to exhibit some aggression towards me about how I was raising our children and made minor complaints about my work hours because he wanted me to be home more. He became unfaithful as a husband. Our house phone rang at all hours of the day, and the person calling hung up as soon as I answered. He became violent with me if I questioned his late-night whereabouts. Once again, the physical abuse began. I felt like I needed to find a safe shelter for me and the children, so after I secured another apartment, I left all the children's clothes and beds behind. I had to start from scratch. I knew if I stayed there, I might not get out alive this time around. I prayed day and night for God to save me and my children. I was in the same cycle I had been in before, but with the Lord on my side, I would not lose. Thank God he stopped attending the church we went to. As for me and the children, we still attend that same church to this day.

My life transitioned once again, from being a married mother of three to becoming a hardworking single mother. With the struggles, obstacles, depression, and nervous breakdown, things were not easy, but I held on with my three children by my side. I had to show strength and courage to be able to get back up again. When I went through the divorce, I remained strong and resilient for my children. I believed God allowed all this to happen because he knew I was strong. I am a soldier in the army of the Lord, and I can do all things through Christ which strengthens me. The Lord knew the plans he had for my life. It was planned well before I was born. God planned everything to get me to where I am today.

As a woman, I am powerful, dynamic, and unique in my own way. I was not a perfect wife, nor a perfect mother, but I would not change my life for anything in the world. With dignity and strength, I raised three great young people. I made some mistakes along the way, but the Lord made my crooked lines straight. For all advisement and correction, I depended on the Lord only, and he never steered me wrong. The Lord turned my hurt and pain into faith, healing, and comfort. He taught me how to forgive myself and others. He taught me how to kick the dust of my shoes and keep moving. The storms in my life were there to make me stronger. My past has refined me for a better future. I thank God for the strength and courage to be able to get back up again. I needed to share this story because I know some young woman is going through the same things I endured. God has more work for me to do.

CHAPTER 13

Unstoppable

MELINDA LEWIS

What it is like being a woman? This is a question that will not have just one simple answer. Your view might not be the same as it is for me. We all manifest womanhood in many different ways, depending on life experiences. I honestly never put too much thought or effort in thinking about this question until I was asked to write about it. My initial encounter of womanhood was complicated for numerous reasons. I became a mother at seventeen, so I once held a different standard and expectation. The world I saw was without grace and had a slight bit of heaviness. I felt ashamed, hurt, and alone. If I can describe what I experienced in a metaphorical way, it was like I had flies in my home that I just could not get rid of. I chose the word "home" it can represent the body. My home and mind were being exposed to something I could not comprehend at first. I knew my life had changed dramatically because I was going to be responsible for someone other than myself, and I was okay with that. I had not one complaint about the duties of a mother. What I did not understand was the amount of intolerance there was in the eyes of older women. There was no fulfillment in the level of support I received when I tried to make decisions to benefit my future. It was insufficient for sure, and I felt less than. I thought my dreams were out of reach. I am not saying I gave up. I just knew I had to take the longer route. I tried to figure out different angles I had to tackle, and this gave me perspective about how life works.

I was blessed to grow up knowing both sides of the family. Everybody went to church, and under the same denomination. You can imagine all the aunties, uncles, and tons of cousins I saw every Sunday. I laugh to myself because I can hear my husband asking, "Are they all your family?" I am blessed because not everybody knows their family, praise God. I witnessed highs and lows with my family, friendships, and relationships. I am a big believer that family is the first foundation and crucial role in social development. What strength and skills we learn from our family can help us conquer any adversity we may face?

What it is like being a woman? Is to not pounder and relive everything that I saw, heard, or been through. I do not say this to demean anyone. As a child, it was all about doing what I was told; "speak no evil, hear no evil". My environment was broken. Due to my parents' separation, my father was absent throughout my childhood. My mother did her best to keep us grounded in church, and we lived a secluded lifestyle. It was not easy for her raising us three children. We stayed with many family members until I was about fifteen, when we found a permanent place.

What it is like being a woman? It is about being able to recognize the bad habits that were holding me back. It is about seeing my own flaws in my reflection, and not just finger pointing at my parents.

What it is like being a woman? It is knowing the difference between life and the cookie-cutter illusion. For me, there was no need to pretend. I saw beyond what I did not have. Did I mature? Sure! I truly give God the glory for not repeating the same negative cycle. Along the way, I saw and dealt with many domineering women who were bullies. I was written off a few times. In the public eye, I saw women scanning for the negative instead of for the good. Sometimes I feel like I grew up in a generation where it was every woman for themselves. The funny thing is that in some households, that cycle is still alive.

What it is like being a woman? It is being a woman who will not demonize another to make herself look victorious. That is what I got out of that. I had to learn not to entertain or tolerate the company of a bitter soul who intentionally misconstrued anything I said, and sometimes things I never said.

What is it like being a woman? It means being able to love from a distance, regardless of the circumstances. I say this humbly and with integrity that no woman is perfect, but every woman can be forgiven. It is one of the effects of being deeply rooted in Christ; being Christ-like. As a woman, I want to share with you how I have handled every stick and stone thrown at me over the years. I have built internal barriers to guard and protect my heart. This comes from my childhood upbringing. For example, my first reaction to just about everyone is to abandon you and reject you in silence, for me to fully appreciate and value your time. If you are a woman who is reading this, you probably are saying to yourself, "she's antisocial" or "she has trust issues". I get it, trust me! Through my entire life, people assumed I disliked them or was secretly judging them because I did not socially engage with them. That was usually the excuse for them not to like me.

What is it like being a woman? It is not a negative thing to ask. Actually, it is an invitation to say what we did not or would not say to our inner self. I am not what some people think. I am extremely social. I enjoy being around my family and others, but just in a selective manner. I am that woman who proudly introduces herself to her neighbors. I once wrote a letter or two because I felt I could express myself better through writing to clear up any misunderstandings. Now there I go again, telling on myself (not everyone is worthy of a letter)! Today, old and new memories have been reestablished through better communication and understanding.

We are everything that God created us to be. By using our challenges, we can upgrade our ways of thinking. If you see it, face it. My experiences have groomed me as a wife, mother, daughter, and sister. I am evolving to that kind of woman I wanted others to see. A loyal woman, like in the Bible story of Ruth; somebody who will stick to you like gorilla glue. A woman who loves with her entire heart and will empathize but will not take sides. That is me for sure. My experiences, good and bad, made me a strong and independent woman.

What is it like being a woman? It is about being honest. I am aware that I do not like to be bothered by people sometimes, especially when my hormones are out of control. I am in tune with my lack of expression; however, I really care too much. I came to terms with that, but I am not the same person I used to be. I am more in tune with my feelings.

What it is like being a woman? It is not just about our hidden scars. It is also about knowing that life is an unknown journey. It is perfectly okay not knowing what lies ahead, but when you hold God's hand during your journey, you will never feel defeated. I am willing to continue changing for the better. Adapting to the curveballs, rather than fighting against them, while I stand in the center of my faith. It was never about what I have, or how much I achieved. I came to terms that not every woman will share the same common interest. As a matter of fact, they may not even like the same air you breathe, but that is ok. Eventually, some of them will start to gasp for air. Sometimes it takes a little longer for some women to realize their worth.

What is it like being a woman? It is about forgiveness. It is about loving your family and friends, even if it is not reciprocated. As a child I use to fish for validation from some family members. There was a time when I felt inadequate, and all I want to do is wear my cape over my face. As a woman, I made my peace and appreciate my past for how it shaped me. My fishing days are over. I have my superwoman cape on now, and I am flying high. People who did not know me often made assumptions that I was impolite, timid, or arrogant. I heard a saying that quiet people always know more than they seem (just give them a chance). Like I said before, it was never difficult to express myself as a woman; it is about not disclosing more than I need to about myself.

Along my journey, I learned not to lean into my own understanding and to acknowledge the righteous path. Even though I shared my somewhat negative experience with other women and the effect my past had on me, I was surrounded by many phenomenal and uplifting women. I call them my sisterhood of friendship. No matter how near or far, we can call each other and say anything without judgment. A real friend will tell you when you are wrong, even when you think you are right. When your vision is narrow, you need a friend to help you see. A handful of family and childhood friends helped me cope during some stressful points in my life. We had each other. They knew my struggles and I knew theirs. I also honor the beautiful friendships made with women I just met. These are the women I would be on the phone within prayer. Or we would just talk, laugh, or have conversations just because I needed to vent. I call them a rainbow of women, but not only because they come from different backgrounds. I quietly watched them as they challenged me from their own experiences. They embraced me and never realized how the roots of my inner beauty needed to be fertilized. Cheering me on with, "Girl, you got this!", the support I am receiving from women I have never met personally is mind-blowing.

What it is like being a woman? I will use a quote by Marie Curie: "You cannot hope to build a better world without improving the individuals. To that end each of us must work for his own improvement, and at the same time share a general responsibility for all humanity, our particular duty being to aid those whom we think we can be most useful." It means being a woman who listens to you when you need an ear, and being a friend for life. I am that woman who will look out for you, and we will look out for each other. I am that woman who loves surrounding myself with loving and trustworthy people. Sometimes we need to revisit the past so we can see our mistakes. We have to believe in ourselves and refuse to give in to our circumstances so easily. They do not define who we are. We let life give us our teachable moments. All the pieces to life's puzzle are far from perfect, but they can come together to create a beautiful masterpiece.

What it is like being a woman? It is about sharing a connection with each woman, despite our differences. Each woman holds a special place in my heart. A strong woman can accept the good and bad of another. We can know about another's hidden struggles and not pass judgment. I noticed that once I committed myself to my goals, I silenced the naysayers. I became more focused on where I wanted to be instead of where I came from. It is about living in my "now". My fears and roadblocks will not get in my way. I try to be more self-aware about all the related traits women have. We are stronger together. I believe that God-given wisdom gives us the capability to bounce off each other's energy. This feels like an "aha!" moment, so I will ask myself one last time. What is it like being a woman? It feels extraordinary. I feel unstoppable. It is about me, Marvelous Melinda, having a celebration that needs no reason.

CHAPTER 14

Breaking The Silence

DINA CAMPOS

I went through hell while I was in school, but I faced it alone and in silence. I was bullied and picked on for trying to do well in school, for dressing and acting differently from the other girls. The funny thing was, I tried fitting in with everyone else because it did not feel good to stand out from the crowd. So, at one Halloween event at school, I put a bag together and took some of my mother's makeup and a short skirt to get dressed up in the school bathroom. I wanted to look like the other girls, to avoid them insulting and mocking me, but it did not help. I trusted one of the girls who offered to do my makeup, but when she had finished I looked in the mirror and my makeup was a mess. I looked like a clown out of a circus. They all laughed and made fun of me, and even called some of the guys over in the hall so they would look at me. I was mortified and changed my clothes and took everything off immediately. Clearly, that was not who I was, and pretending to be someone else made me look foolish in front of everyone. All these experiences affected me, I would dread going to school but I did not know how to let my parents know about the culture I was exposed to in school. All the pressure to fit in was so much that, eventually, I started failing in all my classes, I would walk out the class, hide in the bathroom and Anger began to overpower me. I was so tired of being bullied, tired of feeling different, and tired of being the girl that someone always said something obnoxious about. I just wanted to make it stop! In case you are wondering, this was middle school for me.

I was relieved to leave middle school, have a fresh start in high school. However, it did not take too long for me to realize, high school was exactly the same if not worse so, I adapted quickly, I was not going to be bullied again. I made some bad choices; I became that girl who skipped classes just to hang out. I became that girl who sneaked alcoholic drinks inside the school and got involved in a very abusive relationship. I was that girl who met the demon of depression, and along with that came a mix of other demons named anxiety, panic, and suicide. Anger was a poison that ran through me. I felt controlled by it. There is a saying that "hurt people hurt people", and this could not be farther from the truth. I knew this was not who I was supposed to be, and this kind of life was not what I wanted but at that time, I wanted to move far from the girl who lived deep down inside. I rejected that sweet, kind, smart girl because she was not accepted by anyone. That girl was broken, that girl was holding some pain inside her, that nobody cared to hear about in school. The girl who I was inside was too nice, too smart, and too much of a caring person to survive high school. Nobody cared about that girl, so I tried to do the popularity thing while in high school and it worked for a short period. I drank, smoked, and dressed like all the girls. People seemed to like and accept me. We had a bunch of fake smiles going around, spreading gossip like wildfire, and shockingly, none of this even mattered to me because I still felt empty and alone. I was not being bullied, but more than ever, I had an identity crisis, I had forgotten who I wanted to be, to become who everyone else wanted to see. When I was alone, I cried my eyes out. I felt ashamed of the person I became, and all for what? Fake friends and fake love? My friends were just a bunch of girls who hated themselves and were confused about their own emotions.

After a while, I realized how right I was. It was all fake. I was not really liked and accepted. I just fit the mold and temporary expectations of others. I was eventually betrayed by one of those girls. She called me her friend and I considered her as a friend. But then I recognized how I was only good enough for her when it was time to ditch class for booze. Other than that, I found myself being alone, I was addicted to numbing my old wounds with booze, and cigarettes so I did not stop. I kept skipping classes, drinking in the parks, alone because my so-called friends did the right thing by going back to class and not drinking anymore, but they left me behind. They did not bother to help me, they stopped talking to me, now I became a bad influence. Can you believe that? Graduation came around and they graduated on time and had prom and it looked like one big fake friendship family. The damage I did to myself caught up with me, I was not able to graduate or go to prom, or have a senior trip. I had to do an extra year of high school with a bunch of students who were estranged from me. On my own. Yes, you read that right. I did not graduate on time. All of these experiences affected my self-esteem, but my family's support helped me to get my life together. Even after all the hell, I put them through, they loved me and helped me get through it. I was in school from morning to night. I had regular classes, afterschool, and night school. My schedule was 8:00am to 8:30pm. It was a tiring, stressful, but also an empowering road. I found strength in me, I was unaware of that, that made it possible to do all of that work. My life changed because of the love and support my family gave me. I slowly learned to love myself for me, and I stopped drinking so much and smoking. As a teenager, I experienced so many emotional changes. But I was also a teenager who was raised in the Christian church. I was taught to have morals and principles. I was raised to carry myself as a respectable young lady by dressing and behaving modestly. I was taught to have a prayer life and to have a relationship with God. These principles shaped me, and they were fundamental to me changing my life around. Of course, going through all I went through I did not see the blessing of being raised that way, instead I felt all eyes were on me to set an example everywhere I went, I put pressure on myself to hold myself in that place of respect, faith, loyalty but This was not acceptable in school, so I pretended to be someone else. As "Miss Goody Two Shoes," I felt like I would have never survived that environment just by being myself. In the process of trying to be someone else and pleasing my fake friends, I lost my identity, I lost sight of who I was and who I wanted to be, I no longer knew who I was, and this feeling of being lost followed me for a very long time. I graduated in my fifth year of high school with a paper that was supposed to make me feel like I was going somewhere, like I had a big future awaiting me, but I was depressed, upset, alone, confused and I still felt like a failure.

I just wanted to turn the pages of all those horrific experiences and be happy. Go to college, find my perfect career but what I found were the skeletons in my closet were not skeletons, they were much alive. All of the pain I thought would go away with time, was making an entrance every time I tried to move on with life and build my future. I was dragging anger and low self-esteem with me year after year. You see it never dawned on me that I had other experiences in my life that were hanging on to me even before middle school came around. I had a skeleton hidden under the bones of all the other experiences I had overcome and defeated. This skeleton was different because it had a name: it was Dante, I remember you, but I did not think you ever would have become a problem for me years later. This is my fourth-grade memory. It was a regular day in school until the bell rang and everyone went to grab their belongings from the closet. I was ready to grab my things, I entered the closet, then you came—bigger than me and taller than me—pushing me deep into the closet and getting on top of me. I felt all your weight on me as you breathed on my neck close to my ear. It was hot and it was horrifying. Your kiss on my cheek was so wet, I felt disgusted. I kicked you in the stomach and ran out as fast as I could to catch up to the class line. My heart was racing as I was running in the hall to get back in line. God was with me! I made it; I was free from you.

It was very hard trying to stay in school that day. I spoke with the teachers and told them what Dante did, all the while trying to reach his face so I could rip his eyes out. The teachers ran and told the principal about what I said...and then came the show. "Let's bring the parents in!", etc. The whole nine yards. By that time, Dante looked confused. He was not going to blatantly admit that he pushed me down to the floor in the closet and started lifting up my shirt and gave me this awful kiss on my cheek, until I was able to escape his devious plans. When our parents arrived, his parents concluded—somehow—that he just wanted to get close to me, that he had some type of mental issue and did not mean to do what he did. It felt like they just ignored everything I first told them. If I did the right thing for speaking up, why was my voice not being heard? Now I'm lost! "Dante has a problem, so we will move him to another class." Whatever. Dante did not seem to have a problem when he calculated how to push me into the closet and attack me before anyone noticed we were missing. My father was ready to roll some heads, but everything was left as it was. Because I was a young girl, who was led to believe it was some misunderstanding, I thought that experience would not have a lasting effect on me. I convinced myself that what everyone said was probably right. I convinced my mind that I made a big deal about it and maybe I should have stayed quiet, but that feeling of being violated grew within me, I felt that what happened was not okay, it was wrong, and secretly me wrestling with him getting away with that created a monster in me that reflected in the years that followed. When I became aware, in middle school through a sex education class of what it meant to be violated, I had an awakening and realized, that kid violated me, it got on top of me, interrupted my personal space touched me, kissed me without consent and got away with it. This was just a ticking bomb waiting to go off, and it did and everything else I went through after that brought so much pain and emotional stress. All the memories, and unresolved pain showed up everywhere. In my ability to make decisions clearly, in my ability to embrace my skills, to speak up, to be alone outside. It affected me in building relationships, trusting people and being around people.

There is no chance to go back in time and give my younger self advice, like being mindful about what you speak because your voice is powerful and can change your life and the lives of those around you. I cannot go back and tell myself to stop wasting time and energy belittling myself, and self-sabotaging every good thing that might come my way. I cannot go back and tell myself to stop believing that I am not smart enough, I am not good enough, I am not pretty enough, and that I do not need to compare myself to those girls in school. I cannot go back and tell myself to stop putting myself down like those girls in school put you down. I cannot go back and tell myself to stop living in pain and in silence. I cannot go back in time to assure myself that what Dante did was wrong, it was not my fault, and he or anybody else does not decide the future I will have. What I can do, and what I did was break the silence so I could live in freedom.

The dark painful reality I once lived, and the battle to keep quiet is finally over. I wondered for years why I did not like to hear my voice, and what was the reason I pulled away from friendships, and collaborations. Why did I want to hide all the time, when deep down I really desired to share, teach, and serve people. I unknowingly carried this belief from my past that if I stay quiet and try to go unnoticed, no one would have anything to judge me for. Even today, as a grown woman, I wrestle with attention being drawn to me. Not even positive attention. I have had some difficulty making friends and collaborating with others because of a lack of trust and because I did not want people to see me, for who I am internally. I grew up in church, so I knew God, but when all these things happened and life started knocking me down, I blamed God. I did not blame Dante's actions. I did not blame the choice he made to treat me the way he did, nor did I place all the blame on those who bullied me, made fun of me, and betrayed me. No, it was God who I blamed because he is all-powerful, and he could have stopped it all. I know I am not the only one who has felt this way before.

It took me years of growth, counseling, internal work, and relationship-building with God to understand this. Life does not happen to us –it happens for us. Yes, God knows all and can do all, but we are responsible for the decisions we make. Where Dante chose wrong, it was Dante's doing, not God's. The beauty of God's word is that it is so soothing and liberating. I was able to find healing through God and through his words. I opened my heart to forgiveness, and to a new life in him so that he could work all things together for my good. It was a process, like just about everything else in life is. In my process, he provided healing and helped to shape my faith and trust in him. My story can now be a beacon of hope and not an unfixable tragedy. I am now a healed woman in the hands of a healing Father. My life has not been exempted from pain and heartache, but God has protected me. He has comforted me. He taught me how to forgive others and embrace a new life in him. I believe all my life experiences brought me here, shaping me to be a woman who walks in freedom and helps other women walk into theirs. I am breaking the silence because the silence no longer has a hold on me. I was a broken, lost young girl. I was a woman who was defined by her past for some time, but that is not who I am anymore. Now I want you to see me, not the old me, but the woman God has made completely new, the real me.

CHAPTER 15

The Weaker Vessel

MONIQUE BROWN FRANCIS

I love being a woman. We are such uniquely and beautifully designed creations of the Master Creator. As I reflected upon my experiences as a woman, the following scripture came to me: "Likewise, ye husbands, dwell with them according to knowledge, giving honor unto the wife, as unto the weaker vessel, and as being heirs together of the grace of life; that your prayers be not hindered" (1 Peter 3:7). In this Bible verse, the apostle Paul refers to the wife, the woman, as the "weaker vessel". Why would he use such language to describe us? After carefully considering and researching the words, I definitely agree that a distinct part of my design is being a vessel. The Merriam Webster Dictionary defines the word 'vessel' as "a container (such as a cask, bottle, kettle, cup, or bowl) for holding something". Twice, I have held a baby in my womb. I have held others' secrets as well as my own. I have even held others' dreams more securely than my own.

Vessels not only hold things; they also serve. Think about a coffee carafe. After it has been filled with freshly brewed coffee, it is used to pour out, to serve. After listening to and being filled with others' ideas, I have been a vessel that poured out support to help those dreams become a reality. After being filled with my own tears, I have poured out compassion and comfort to hurting souls. After being filled to the brim with hurt, I learned how to pour out grace, mercy, and forgiveness upon those who caused my pain. Yes, we are vessels who serve a great purpose, so why then are we described by Paul as "weaker" vessels? I could understand if he had simply used the word "weak". Everyone gets weak sometimes, but Paul uses a comparative adjective, "weaker", instead. Would that suggest that husbands – men—are weak too. Being a woman, I am not able to speak about what makes men weak, but I can certainly highlight some things that are apt to make women weak.

Disappointments make us weak. It is disappointing to share our dreams with people who fail to catch our vision or support us as we pursue bringing the vision to fruition. Infidelity makes us weak. We are devastated to learn that a partner had an indiscretion after loving him fervently and trusting him completely. Abuse in any form—mental, emotional, financial, verbal, or physical—makes us weak. A swollen eye weakens our sight. A joint bank account that has been emptied out by a spouse weakens our ability to pay bills and make necessary purchases. Being told that you are not good enough, or to the other extreme, *not* being told that you are *more* than enough, creates low self-perception and weakens our ability to love others as well as ourselves. Not being held, kissed, or made love to makes us weak, liable to yield to temptation, and driven to find that which we lack in the arms of another.

These are some of the issues, circumstances, and experiences that make us weak, but Paul uses the word "*weaker*" when referring to the woman, which is translated as "strengthless", "more feeble", and "without strength". I can say that at times I have been rendered "more feeble" due to circumstances, conditions, or experiences. There were times when my bills were greater than *both* bank account balances combined. There were days that I did not want to go to work because I was tired from having been oppressed, mistreated, and ostracized. There were moments when I just couldn't take another betrayal, couldn't take another person slandering or scandalizing my name. However, I have learned, and can therefore affirm, that we are actually much stronger than many realize. As women, our strength is not connected only to our physical being or measured simply by our physical prowess. Our strength is not determined by how much we can bench press. Our strength lies in how much we can hold up, and hold in, and hold onto under pressure. I have staggered under the weight of silence as I carried the knowledge of others' scandals, misdeeds, and shortcomings. But I did not collapse under the strain because I was determined to preserve family, marriage, ministry, and relationships.

Earlier in this chapter, I shared one definition of the word "vessel", but there is another. Again, referencing the Merriam Webster Dictionary, a vessel is "a person into whom some quality (such as grace) is infused". Upon looking at me, many would not be able to see with their natural eye that I have experienced and sustained a great deal of hurt, pain, and trauma, but God infused into me His grace to survive and to stand. Not only does God infuse grace; he also infuses his love, wisdom, and Spirit. He infuses hope and optimism. He infuses truth and integrity. These are virtues that we, the "weaker" vessel, hold and contain within. Thus, in all reality, those virtues make us stronger, not weaker. I have worked and served with people who took my humility and kindness for weakness. Some have done me wrong. Others tried to take further advantage of me because I did not react by cursing them out or doing something worse. They pushed a little harder, they nudged a little deeper. Some days I was low in spirit. I may have bent but would not, and *did not*, break! We, the "weaker vessel", have strength of character and strength in spirit. We may be at our breaking point and feel like giving up, but we do not.

I submit that we, the "weaker" vessel, are in fact stronger when we do not give in to others' taunts, or crumple into a heap when people hurl epithets and insults at us. The tasks presented before us may be daunting, and life's challenges may seem insurmountable. But we will not back down; we will not quit. This type of vessel will not abandon the assignment of loving her children, supporting her husband, and serving her God.

What is it like being a woman? For me, it is being fearless in the thick of adversity. Even when my knees are knocking, I will never let them see me sweat. I square up and turn out! But I am not alone. I am not the only woman professional who completes that report by its deadline. I am not the only mother who can create a meal with only six ingredients to ensure that my family eats. We make countless sacrifices, putting the needs of others before our own so that they may prosper. What is it like being a woman? It is persevering in the hardest trials when you most feel like giving up. It is being tenacious and diligent about completing tasks and achieving goals. People look at us and wonder how we do it. Some look at us and judge us without knowing our story, but oh if they did, they would marvel at how we are standing, how we are thriving, and how we are smiling in spite of obstacles and heartaches. It is the working of God and the Holy Spirit that causes us to be strong, that causes us to triumph over people, over circumstances, and over our woes because of the strength that they have infused into us.

The "weaker" vessel actually becomes the stronger vessel when she chooses to accept the Lord Jesus Christ as her personal Savior and enters into a real, bona fide relationship with Him. She is a stronger vessel when she puts her hope, trust, and faith in God. She is empowered when she submits her will to God and yields herself to the Holy Spirit to receive his guidance, correction, and grace. I can attest to this because this is what happened to me when I established a relationship with Jesus Christ. The only way to receive all these necessary and vital qualities is to open ourselves to the Father. It can be difficult to do this when we have suffered betrayals and crushing blows by the ones we trusted, revered, and loved the most. As I was once challenged, I now challenge you to examine the numerous people you opened your heart, your home, and your body to, and ask yourself: "Why *not* open yourself to the Father?" Give God a chance to pour into and fill you. Let him replace your hurts and be a salve to your wounds. Allow God the opportunity to infuse his essence into you, his beautiful vessel and beautiful woman.

At first, I was a bit jolted by Paul's label and reference to us as the weaker vessel, but now, I celebrate being a woman even more because I know how much purpose and value I hold. We are vessels of honor! The next time you experience low morale, pressure, or attack from an external force, renew your strength with the knowledge that you are "fearfully and wonderfully made" by a loving Creator who fashioned you with all uniqueness in all of his glory. Weakness is not a fault or failure. *All* human beings, regardless of gender or age, experience moments of weakness. When we experience those moments, it is an opportunity for God to build and empower us. It is an opportunity for him to not only endow us with strength, but to *be* our Strength. As vessels infused by God's strength, we are able to be strong for others who are weak. Remember that we are remarkable women. We serve multiple purposes and fulfill many roles. We have great impact! We should never once doubt our strength, value, or worth. We should never stop being filled up so we can pour out. The rewards are immeasurable!

CHAPTER 16

Growth And Maturity

PINKIE FARMER

What is it like to be a woman? Maturity is the first thing that came to mind. A mature female moves through the natural stages of development: infant, child, adolescent, teenager, and then adult. After reaching adulthood, the journey of a woman evolves many times over. After graduating from high school at eighteen years old, I was a young woman now working as a clerk typist at a Social Security office in Bristol, Virginia. The excitement of being independent was great and challenging. I realized my mother would not be waking me up in the morning, so I bought a "Big Ben Double Bell" clock to ensure I would wake up timely. Much to my surprise, I was always on time. I enjoyed my time working in Bristol, where one side of the street was in Virginia, and the other side was in Tennessee. It was here that I bought clothes for the first time on my own. The next hurdle I faced was cooking dinner for myself. Thank goodness, Swanson TV dinners were in business. At least I knew how to shop and follow the box directions. After a while, I wanted some kale and mustard greens. At least this was something I could handle. I just had to clean them and cook them. I survived by cooking things on a very small scale.

A few years later, I relocated back to Richmond, Virginia, my hometown. After being on my own, a rude, disheartening awakening happened. My mother resumed her duties. Washing my clothes became a thing of the past. Cooking? That was out. That independent part of my life was gone! Living with my parents as an adult was far different than when I was a child. Even though I was an adult, I was still a "child" who had to obey their house rules.

Now being a young woman in my twenties, I found myself pleasing others. I lived by the idea motto "Jesus first, others next, yourself last". I would not speak up for myself. Then one hot summer day as I waited in the car while some relatives shopped in the mall, I was very late arriving at a church service that I wanted to go to in town. I decided it was time for me to start taking care of myself. I began reading self-help books that gave me insight for improvement.

While still in my twenties, I got married and experienced more growth. My husband was quite an outspoken person. He was strong-willed, kind-hearted, and he loved God. When he found out I could not cook, he quickly bought me a thick "Cookbook Encyclopedia." I knew how to follow recipes, which was a great help. We had many delicious dishes, and neither one of us ever got sick! I was flexible, always ready to learn and improve my cooking skills.

It is during this period that I began to appreciate who I was as a woman. I found myself being a peacemaker during times of confusion and misunderstanding. There were times I held my lips together gently, but tightly. It is very difficult when you are the one who is wrong, or when you do not understand. This was the time where God became the only one I turned to. God was near. He helped me by giving me peace in my mind, and a song in my heart. With God's help, I was able to see the good when things got rough. As I learned to let my husband be the head of the home, it was then that he began to ask me for advice more often. That was a big victory for life!

Now in my seventies, I enjoy being a woman who has more wisdom and continues to get more understanding about things. It is best to keep evolving, to keep learning, and to keep growing. This is what life is all about, but it is difficult to go through life without Christ. He is always near, even when you do not think he is. As women, the weaker vessels, we have an underlying strength that God gave us. He gave us the ability to see beyond what is visible. What we like to say is that we know what we know, even when we cannot explain how we know. God surprises us by helping us understand certain situations. Leaning on God gives me peace and strength. When we come through problems, it causes us to be stronger in knowing how real God is. Without the problem, there is no growth in God. I learned to thank Him for the lessons, good and bad. Oh, how it made me better in God as well. I can face a situation knowing, letting, and expecting God to handle it.

Being a woman means me being Christ-like, dainty, neat, quiet, kind, loving, caring, soft-spoken, calm, happy, smiling, helping, problem-solving (depending upon what the problem is), and flexible to make do with what I have. But on the other hand, when the enemy shows his ugly head, I stand up with the belt of truth on my waist, the shoes of the gospel of peace on my feet, the breastplate of right doing covering my chest, the helmet of salvation covering my head to keep my thoughts on the right track, the shield of faith to stop the enemy's darts of fire against me, the sword of God's word, and with much prayer.

Women were made by a loving and caring God who hears and helps us if we acknowledge him. In creation, everything God made was good, and I am included. It is with assurance that I know God made me an amazingly wonderful woman. I honor, love, and adore God for making me who I am, and for who you are: SPECIAL.

CHAPTER 17

I Am Splendid

ROBIN DODSON

I am splendid. My heart finally smiles as I embrace the totality of femme, gal, matron, me. This girl with the long, wavy hair and big hips who embraces every imperfection and stretchmark. This sister girl who rebounded from mental abuse and tremendous scandal with more twists than a movie or a sitcom. This girl who endured exposure that was intended to crush her, but had a swanky exodus from the epithetical into how she is splendid.

This journey emerged as a consequence of an enormous, bruised heart being subjugated. In my mid-twenties, I was a blushing bride, and it was a great milestone for a black woman to marry her children's father. My family was a photo-perfect model of exquisiteness. Yes, I dared and unaware, saying "I Do" gave an assailant legal permission to plunge my heart. Now I am a woman sleeping and loving an enemy. That enemy, that husband, that man tried to crush me. Me, that wife, this mother, this woman. His words were degrading. He always prioritized his time elsewhere, but his demand for sex could never be denied. That wife was dedicated to serving. The old school way of thinking prevailed: submit, cook, and clean. That man's icy complaints were forever present. That enemy never wanted me to feel adequate, and the masses revered me to his displeasure. People adored my presence, style, and confidence –and it made him ferocious.

In my mid-thirties, I birthed two more angels and remained faithful to my torn vows. That enemy's mangled words backfired, but the adultery tore up my entrails. Rumors of pregnancy, hotel shenanigans, bewitchery, and other transgressions with women went into my ears. One stabbing betrayal after another induced heart hemorrhage, an emotional pain that could either make me or break me. There were only two ways to travel: the road to deep depression, or the road to self-discovery, the road that saved my life. With self-discovery rooted in me, I triaged, assessed, and mended my wounds. From the roof of self-discovery, my determination blossomed.

In my mid-forties, I embraced the thought of leaving my enemy by traveling through the valley of divorce. I became a homeless single mother and a caregiver to a disabled sister. Being penniless, I stayed with a girlfriend for a few months and made my bed on her floor. Although I was in ecumenical survival mode, I soaked up this scripture: "I praise you because I am fearfully and wonderfully made; your works are wonderful, I know that full well." (Psalm 139:14 NIV). That word infused divine strength into me. God fearfully, extremely, exceedingly, and passionately created me, despite human beings' neglect. That scripture reinforced the thought that I am a wonderment of God's divine penmanship. As a Word girl, I let the scriptures reverberate loudly in my ears:

> [26]*Then God said, "Let us make mankind in our image, in our likeness, so that they may rule over the*

fish in the sea and the birds in the sky, over the livestock and all the wild animals, and over all the creatures that move along the ground. [27]So God created mankind in his own image, in the image of God he created them; male and female he created them. [28]God blessed them and said to them, "Be fruitful and increase in number; fill the earth and subdue it. Rule over the fish in the sea and the birds in the sky and over every living creature that moves on the ground.

Genesis 1:26-28 NIV

Knowing this for myself caused me to dance, chiefly in understanding how God creates masterful things where darkness resides. His breathe moves throughout my soul, causing me to sing the anthem that I am to be fruitful. I am to subdue, rule, and manage my earthly assignment so I can produce an authentic sound throughout the earth.

---

[30]Then will appear the sign of the Son of Man in heaven. And then all the peoples of the earth will mourn when they see the Son of Man coming on the clouds of heaven, with power and great glory. [31]And he will send his angels with a loud trumpet call, and they will gather his elect from the four winds, from one end of the heavens to the other.

Matthew 24:30-31 NIV

This bold teaching about the Son of Man returning upon the clouds of heaven with trumpets blaring resonates in my spirit. I found my cloud, and I make a grand and thunderous entrance whenever I enter a room. The sound of my trumpet is so loud that it cannot be ignored. I am created in God's image. I am a trailblazer who cannot be overlooked. I am splendid! This declaration became my personal affirmation and lifeline to dispel every fabrication against me. I am beautiful, and I am worthy of authentic love. This splendid woman is a successful entrepreneur, philanthropist, motivational speaker, and so many other things. I am fearfully and wonderfully made. I am a wonderment of God's divine penmanship who defied darkness in my life. I am riding my cloud, making a grand, thunderous entrance wherever I go, and my trumpet calls for attention. I am splendid!

CHAPTER 18

Black Butterfly

CHAUNCY A. HENERY

Butterflies have fascinated me ever since I was a little girl. One would never think that an unattractive, unassuming caterpillar would be transformed into such a majestic, colorful and beautiful insect. Although I love them all, monarch butterflies are my favorite. Butterflies develop through a process called *metamorphosis*, which in the Greek means "transformation" or "change". Depending on the species of butterfly, the transformation can take from five to twenty-one days. Like these beautiful insects, every woman has a process coupled with life experiences that transform her into her better and best self. If you look at me now, it might be hard to fathom that I was once a painfully shy little girl who, as she grew older, learned to mask her insecurities throughout her adolescence then subsequently into adulthood. I saw myself as being more like the unassuming caterpillar than the graceful butterfly.

I was born in Guyana, South America to an unwed mother. I was raised by my loving grandparents, Oscar and Althea Semple, for a short time until I migrated to America to join my mother, Doreen, at age four. Subsequently, my mother got married but would later divorce. By that time, I was no longer an only child. I had become the eldest child, now having two younger sisters that looked up to me. We had a good childhood with a lot of love. Throughout my childhood, I was thought of as being quiet, responsible, well-mannered, obedient, and a good student. But no one, including myself, noticed the subtle insecurities building up within me that would ultimately challenge, stretch, and be used to transform me from caterpillar into butterfly.

While growing up, not only was this caterpillar shy, but I saw myself as ugly (a word that I later forbid in my classroom as a special needs educator because I have firsthand knowledge of the emotional scars it causes). The ugly label was also given to me by my peers in school. I involuntarily consented to it with timidity and insecurity. Though I was not unattractive, I began to resent being brown skinned. I found it easy to be critical of my body type, my full lips, and my 4c hair texture. Being mocked and teased about my shyness and looks by bullies throughout elementary and junior high school became the norm. I had wished that God made me bolder with lighter skin and hair that was not only softer but longer. On top of all that, I also questioned God as to why I was named Chauncy (a masculine name, lovingly chosen by my godmother Enid). My name was always mispronounced, and those unfamiliar with my gender would joke about expecting to meet a boy instead of a girl. I could not empathize with whatever they felt was supposed to be humorous about that. Though, I later grew to love my name, I had other insecurities that still plagued me for years.

Throughout my adolescence, I remained shy. I became more adept at masking and internalizing a negative perception of my body image, while having a greater struggle with self-confidence. In high school, I always wore long skirts all year round. It was not because of my Christian beliefs. It was because I thought my legs were too thick and my hips were too wide. I did not want anyone to notice my curvaceous figure. However, I did want to be noticed by the popular kids and to be thought of as one of the cool kids. But with my timid demeanor, soft-spoken voice, and awkwardness, it was evident that no one would see me that way. I was more known for my academic excellence than for my social skills. Those same hurdles would remain challenges well into my adulthood until catalysts of change intervened.

Before the metamorphosis of the caterpillar into an adult butterfly is complete, a critical "resting stage" occurs in the process. This is where a chrysalis is formed to encase the insect while it grows wings and changes into an adult. This stage of the process takes time and cannot be force or interrupted. In 1988, prior to beginning my freshman year to Brooklyn College, I had to undertake a series of placement tests. One of those tests was conducted by the Speech Department to determine the appropriate speech course needed to meet the requirements of their CORE curriculum. To my shock and dismay, it was a verbal test. When it was my turn to be tested, I sat before the department head with what felt like the biggest lump in my throat. She asked me a series of questions about my future aspirations. To my surprise, I answered every question fluently, like a seasoned orator. When our dialogue was over, I was all the more shocked and surprised. I was exempted from taking any speech courses! She wished me well in my future academic endeavors and complimented me on my grammar, poise and self-confidence. At that moment, my self-confidence sky-rocketed. The joy on my face would have made one think that I had just won the lottery!

Another boost to my self-confidence and self-perception about my looks came while I casually watched the Oprah Winfrey Show one day. On this particular show, her guest was a popular author/life coach who gave the studio and viewing audience an assignment. We were to write a letter to ourselves, depicting how we truly felt about ourselves. The letter was solely for us and not to be shared with anyone else. We were to re-read the letter out loud to ourselves while standing in front of a mirror. I completed my multi-page letter and followed the instructions explicitly. Standing in front of my mirror, I could not believe what I heard as I read. It was tearfully painful hearing those false perceptions and erroneous projections coming out of my mouth. How could I think and feel that way about myself? That letter served as the catalyst to help me begin the process of purging and releasing those impure and toxic thoughts. I repented to God and tore that letter up. After doing so, it was if a dam broke, shackles were loosed, and I could fully exhale. For the first time in my life, I saw myself through clearer lens. I heard my voice without the echoes of harsh self-criticism playing over and over in my mind. The black butterfly was now emerging from her chrysalis with boldness, and self-assurance.

The most transformative experience of my life came in 1997, when I accepted Jesus Christ as my Lord and Savior. That life altering choice has helped this former caterpillar transform into a graceful, beautiful, powerful, and extraordinary black butterfly. Inner growth and change begin when you have the courage and confidence to face your truth unapologetically. That is the only way that the better and best "you" can be birthed out. Caterpillars are not ugly; they are just in the early stage of their transformation. Caterpillars are at the beginning of a metamorphosis which births forth that which is unexpected, unique, purpose-filled, and beautiful. Every butterfly has a testimony. Butterflies do not look like where they came from. But their majestic wings take them to where they need to be. This lovely black butterfly is not ashamed of who she was but boldly embraces who she is becoming because I know that I am fearfully and wonderfully made in the image and likeness of God. From head to toe, I love and accept who Chauncy is. The wind beneath my wings, leads me where God needs me to go. "I praise you because I am fearfully and wonderfully made; your works are wonderful, I know that full well." (Psalm 139:14). I shall walk and not faint. I shall run and not be weary. For like an eagle, this black butterfly spreads her wings and soars.

CHAPTER 19

Walking

CARMEN Y. SHOREY

On Sept. 29, 1994, I made my way to work at Tropicana Products. It was a sunny day. After I clocked in and started walking up the stairs to my workstation, one of the steps suddenly gave way. I fell through and I injured my ankle. I was much heavier at that time, so I could feel the pain when I landed on the floor on my ankle. Someone took me to the nurse's station, where I was told I had a bad ankle sprain. They subsequently sent me back to work that same day. I kept having problems with the same ankle, but I continued going back and forth to work, day by day. I went back to the nurse's station because my ankle was getting worse, but this time, I was persistent in letting them know that my ankle was not right. Instead of the pain easing up, I had more of it. It was after many complaints that the nurse finally sent me to a workman's compensation doctor. That doctor continued to tell me that I just had a sprained ankle. So, believing the doctor and not knowing any better, I continued going to work day by day. As my ankle continued to swell and became more painful, I went for a second opinion. It was after seeing a doctor in Sarasota, Florida that, upon getting x-rays, I was told that my ankle had been broken all along. After the x-rays were done, and my ears tingled and my heartrate went up, wondering what the doctor was going to tell me. What I did not want to hear is he told me. I had to have surgery on my ankle as soon as possible. My immediate response was to burst into tears!

The following week, I went to the outpatient clinic to register for the surgery and do paperwork. Imagine my shock when the doctor told me this would be a major surgery. It turns out I walked a full year on that ankle, thinking it was just sprained. Because of that, my ligaments were damaged, and the doctor said all he could do was to try to put them back together. Again, I got very emotional, but I held back my tears. I knew I just had to prepare myself for the surgery. After the surgery was done and I woke up from the anesthesia, the first thing I saw was the condition of my ankle! As I laid there, I looked up and saw my leg in a sling. I had feelings of disappointment and hurt. My whole life had just taken a complete turn from what I expected at that point in time. My thoughts began to overwhelm me: as a mother, how was I going to take care of my son? For that matter, who would take care of me when I went home? When that time came, I called one of my aunts and she really stepped in! I was able to concentrate on my recovery while she took care of my son. It meant a lot for me to be a woman in such a weak condition to be able to reach out to another who could be strong for me.

When I got well enough, I had to start going to a rehabilitation center. For more than two years, this place became my second home. During that time, I had to re-learn walking. I went to therapy in a wheelchair every other day for two and a half years. Everything from my ankle breaking, to the surgery, and now through long-term rehab, caused me to have a mental breakdown. I thought of myself as strong woman, but while in that wheelchair, I had to depend on others for my basic needs. Things like going to the bathroom, taking a shower, getting dressed, and getting in and out of bed could no longer be taken for granted. That depression led to anxiety attacks.

Because of the anxiety, I soon had to see a psychiatrist weekly. The psychiatrist's diagnosis of my situation was clinical depression, along with insomnia. His remedy was to put me on many psych meds such as Xanax, Klonopin, Prozac, and Lexapro. With all this "help", this strong woman had a couple more breakdowns. I could not deal with being unable to walk, so I began to let myself go. My weight went up and I became bigger than I wanted to be. I was at the point where I did not care about life anymore.

After I had those last breakdowns, I became so depressed that I was admitted to the mental ward at the hospital. That would be the next two years of my life spent getting treatment and counseling. With me not caring about myself for all that time, I kept gaining more weight. Because I was not able to work, the hit to my finances took its toll. I fell behind in my bills, and the initial workman's compensation were not enough to help me. Even though I was still in a wheelchair, I was finally able to go home. I was not able to care for myself properly, so workman's compensation sent a certified nursing assistant to my home every day. She helped with showering myself, cleaning, and cooking. I was home now. I could see my car in the driveway. Just looking at it sit there without me being able to drive it just made my depression worse. I had to be driven to my appointments in the accessible van. This was a long, drawn-out situation in my life. As a woman, I felt so ashamed and embarrassed that I got overweight and had to be taken back and forth by the accessible van.

A turnaround for me came one day when my aunt brought my son home to see me. He spoke words to me that I will never forget. He simply said, "Mommy, I miss you!" It was these words that made me realize that I had to get my life together. I had to get myself back on track, and believe me; it was not easy at all. I was so broken down in my body, my heart, and in my mind. But I had to press my way through for my son's sake. That is what being a woman was about for me. His father was not in the picture anymore. My son was my heart. I had to ask God to help me with my situation so that I could become humble and get my thinking right. My mind was so messed up at that time. I even thought of suicide. I prayed to God and asked him to heal me from depression, and from anything that could hinder my life or stop me from bettering myself. In my weakness, my God made me strong. Today, I am walking, talking, and telling my story about God's grace. I know what it is like being a woman through my tests and trials. Without faith, trusting and believing God, I do not know where I would be at this point in my life. Life is so precious. With God, I have overcome so many obstacles in my life. I give God all the glory and the praise.

CHAPTER 20

A Taught Woman

JESSICA FRANCOIS JOHNSON

I am an experienced woman. I learned the hard way that life has not always been trouble-free. I look at my face, day in and day out. Year in and year out. On some days, my face seems clear. And on other days, I might see a pimple. The next year, I might have black heads on my face, and then after a couple years, I see some kind of spot on my face. What is that? Is that an age spot? This is what it has been like for me. As the years go on, I notice how I am getting pains here and there in my body, even as I get out of the bed. Nobody ever told me that part! My great-grandmother used to say, "Just keep going to bed and getting up." Now, I am a firm believer in what she told me. Some mornings, I get out of the bed swiftly, and then there are days where I pour out of bed slower than molasses.

My little sister encouraged me to start walking (she knew I did not like anything harder than that!). My sister-in-law also motivated me to do more of the same. As I started walking more often, I was challenged by a friend to do even more walking. I accepted all challenges with no problem. I walked every day for a month without a day off. But then the day came when my knee started aching while I was enjoying one of my walks. My little sister suggested that I have a doctor check me out. I told you about what it is like for me being a woman. It is not always about the glitz and glamor of some woman you might see walking down the street. As time comes and goes, our bodies start to change. Our figures might expand. We are not always going to look the same; still, we are women. But yeah, let me get back to speaking about myself. My figure expanded over the years. It went from a pear shape to an apple shape.

As a growing child, my hair was considered short. It once reached just above shoulder length. My hair was not really short, but it was not as long as everybody else's. One day when I sat under the hairdryer getting a wrap, I lifted the dryer up and told my sister to cut my hair off. My mother always said that hair doesn't make you a woman. The relationship that I have with my mother taught me a lot about being a woman. I was raised by my mama, Eula Hunter Franklin, in Baton Rouge, Louisiana. I come from a strong group of women. I cannot tell you much at all about my father, but I can tell you about the mama who raised me. She taught me how to pray, how to cook, and how to take care of a family. Mama also taught me how to dress and act like a lady. I enjoyed going to Goudchaux's, where she shopped for finer clothes and hats for church. I always said when I grow up, I will be wearing hats to church like mama did for holidays. Well, that is not true because it was always hard for me to find hats to fit my head! My mother encouraged me to go to school, even though she did not finish high school. She made it to the twelfth grade but did not graduate.

Because of my height and weight, I did not always love myself while I grew up. The women on my mother's side of the family had wide shoulders and were tall. I was a late bloomer. I had short hair, and was tall and very slim during my early years. Growing up in our neighborhood at Capital City South Apartments, I was almost the tallest girl and was teased often because of my long legs. It was my mother who always encouraged me by telling me that I am beautifully and wonderfully made. She is the woman who taught me how to pray and when to pray. She is my prayer warrior. I can go to her with everything going on in my life. She was not pleased with some things I told her, but she would pray for me if she was not praying with me. I remember telling her that I did not know how to pray. I thought I had to sound like the ladies we heard praying in church. Mama told me that praying is talking to God, and all I needed to do was open my mouth and speak to him like I was speaking to her. It took me a very long time to become comfortable with myself praying, but I stopped worrying about how I sounded. With her encouragement, I just prayed.

As a young girl, mama taught me how to cook. When it was time to cook, I stayed in the kitchen to watch and learn. Today, my children tell me that the only foods I cook better than my mother are red beans, meatloaf and peach cobbler. We enjoy baking together, which is one of her favorite things to do. More than ever, I enjoy being in the kitchen with my mother because I know that we are making memories. Mama will not always be here. She also never left the house in a mess. She taught me how to separate clothes, how to wash them by hand and dry them on a clothesline. Oh my! Can I tell you how much I enjoyed that? Going to my great grandmother's house was a great time. When it was time to hang the clothes out, Mama Goldie said, "I am not using that electricity. We are going to catch that sun!." By the time I was pregnant with my first child, I loved hanging clothes on the line so much that Mama Goldie told me to be careful hanging my clothes before I end up tying my baby's umbilical cord around its neck!

My mother said that she used to hear people say that two women cannot live in the same house together. They would say how there would not be any getting along. Mama and I proved them wrong because we have the absolute best relationship living together. I do also credit that I have lived together with her for so long. At times, mama and I can literally finish each other's sentences. And sometimes we find ourselves saying the same thing at the same time. I had two failed marriages, and society has taught us to be ashamed of a failed marriage. Despite what society says, I am not ashamed, but at the end of my second marriage, I felt like I was such a disappointment to my family. My mother assured me that I did all I could do in both marriages. It was not okay for me to beat myself up about it. During each divorce, there was a struggle in trying to act like everything was alright. I went to work every day and never let anybody see me cry. I rarely missed days from work, except for when I had to do filings. Those were hard times, but I had a praying mother. By the time of my second divorce, I could not look my mother in the eyes. My mother never put me down or beat me with unkind words because neither of my marriages didn't work. She wanted me to be happy. There was no way to be happy by staying in a bad marriage just for your child/ren, so I did not. For a couple months, I came home from work and went straight to my room without making face-to-face contact with anybody. I stayed on one side of the house so I would not have to come out and have my mother facing me. Lord knows it was hard even facing my children. After each divorce, I moved back home with my mother. Despite the shame, I am grateful that she allowed me to. That is where I can honestly say that I received strength to not give up on life and treat divorce like it was the end of the world for me and my children. When I tell you it was really a struggle, believe that.

Can I tell you about my s/hero, my mother? During my second divorce, my mother nourished me back to health, physically and mentally. I was a correctional officer at the time getting off work at three-thirty in the afternoon every day, and my days off were every other weekend. She allowed me to come home from work, go straight to my room, bathe, and then jump into bed. Mama would have my evening coffee set by my bedroom door, and then she placed my dinner tray there afterwards. She came back later to get the tray because I still had no strength to face her. This went on for about two to three months. I felt like my second divorce was my fault. My heart ached so bad. I did not want to wake up on some days. But I remember the day when I came from work and instead of going straight to my room, I went to the den where mama was watching TV by herself. When she saw me, she held me tight and yelled out, "There's my baby!" I cried and told Mama how sorry I was that my second marriage did not work out. She immediately started praying to God that I would pull myself together. She kept telling me that it was going to be alright. Well, guess what? Mama said I looked so pitiful, it broke her heart to see me that way. From that day forward, I no longer came home from work feeling ashamed and running straight to my bedroom. This is when our coffee bonding kicked in. We had coffee in the morning and in the evening together. This is one of the favorite things I enjoy with my mother. Y'all talking about peace! It was a peace that came to me because I had a praying mother who taught me to keep pressing on. I will continue making memories with her, and I am grateful for her. I am a taught woman because of what mama said.

CHAPTER 21

Awakening My Voice

SHAYYA ROSETTE

Being women, our voices reveal to us our confidence, our wisdom, and most of all, our power. Once we close off our minds to what others think about us, say about us, and how they treat us, it ultimately leaves room for our most inner voices to be made known. As a young girl, I spent my time doing just as I was told and going where my parents directed me to go, as many of us did. I understood that as children, parents ultimately have to make decisions for us and decide our path until we are of age and can decide for ourselves. They are essentially our voice during our childhood. For example, a child who is in the foster care system has no voice in any matter, and the state decides and speaks for them. Once a child is placed in a home, they have no voice until caseworkers ask them, "How do you like your new home?" They may hesitate to answer that question because "maybe" this could be the *right* home. They may not want to stand the chance of being uprooted and have to keep answering the same questions somewhere else. Here is another scenario: perhaps, as a child, you endured your parent's divorce, and you could not scream and tell them how you felt. You may have thought to yourself, "What they feel is what they feel, but what about me?" Not your place, so you quiet yourself and keep still.

Or remember when you partnered up with someone on an assignment, and the other person took the credit for what you did? You may have asked yourself, "Should I say something?" Did you take the chance of standing up and asserting yourself, or did you think that they would think you were being difficult? Shhh!! Again, like a child, you quiet yourself. Or how about that relationship that was everything you thought it could be at first, but then you started to notice red flags. But you thought how maybe just this once, this could be the one. You thought it might just be a rough patch, and you really did not want to start dating again...so you stayed silent. Your silence continued for years until you felt trapped, and by then, you did not know whether to leave or keep staying.

Or how about going through things like that and then becoming a mother and having your own little girl. You tell yourself that she will not endure what you endured, and she will have all things you did not have. And so on. And what about those times throughout your life when you were asked some of these questions:

"When are you going back to school?"
"When are you having children?"
"When are you going to get married?"
"Why should we hire you?"

The questions can be endless and daunting. It gets our minds wondering about what the answers could or should be. Our responses could be long and drawn out, or answered with a question to redirect the conversation. Because of societal norms, being a woman can be especially challenging at times. The status of "homemaker" is phasing out because more women are moving into the workplace while still juggling personal responsibilities to establish a proper work and life balance. Children are told what to do, how to behave, and how to respond. Do they really even have a voice? In my childhood, the answer was no, not really. I always heard the phrase about staying in a child's place, but what was that place, per se? Is it quiet and still, or is it a loud place where anything goes? Did your family communicate with meetings and open door/floor policy? Or perhaps you grew up in a household where there was a lack of communication, and when it did happen, there was a lot of screaming and fighting? You may have felt like you barely existed. Those are two different places that our childhoods may exemplify. Living in one place, we may not understand someone coming from the other place. As women, we witness the first relationship of our parents. It is the root of how we display and voice our womanhood. I am here to tell you about how my voice was birthed.

Doing the will of God, while finding and coming into your own voice, can be a daunting process. Throughout my life, I heard people say "trust the process" all the time. I feel compelled to share an area of my life where God revealed himself to me, and when I felt my own natural voice had been squashed and rendered useless. There may be some of you have been told you could not do this or that, that you are not enough, and so on. Those negative words and the emotions attached to them could stifle any voice. Then something you never saw coming hits you with so much pain that it was like you were hit by a truck and had the wind knocked out of you. Knocked down to the ground, you felt weak. You tried to speak, but the only thing that flowed out of you was tears. This could have been a broken relationship, marriage troubles, or some other type of rejection. This could have even come from your parents or your children.

All these things can bring a woman to her knees, asking "Why?!" through her tears. During such a hard time in my life, I asked the same thing over and over. I sat in my prayer closet, crying in sorrow and not knowing who I was. My voice was literally lost from trying to get people around me to listen and understand me. Then one day, I looked up, and the tears stopped. God spoke to me, telling me that he understood me and is always listening to me. Psalm 121:1-2 says: "I will lift up mine eyes unto the hills, from whence cometh my help. My help cometh from the LORD, which made heaven and earth." I told myself how I will look to the hills where my help comes from, where my power comes from, where my confidence comes from, and most of all, knowing that my voice comes from the Lord. Then I had a thought: instead of asking why something is happening to me, why not ask whether God is trying to teach me something?

God gave us power and authority to decree and declare things over our lives. We can command things in us that go against what God wants for us to depart and never return again. The awakening of my own voice spiritually transformed me in ways I never would have imagined. It allowed me to think back to those times in my life when I listened to the wrong voices in my head. I thought about how I let what others did and said to me dictate how I lived my life. I started to think and speak differently, using my voice for God's glory. I am so elated to share with other women how the very essence of me speaking my mind and saying what I will and will not do or tolerate is my power. That power is yours too. There is power in your voice, even when people want to stifle it or change it for their own benefit. I am grateful for God showing me that my voice can be heard, even in silence and stillness. Even in my quiet time, I am giving the world my voice.

I surprise myself in how I use discernment about things that used to get an immediate reaction out of me. Now, I use wisdom when confronted with people's actions and situations. I remind myself that not every situation deserves a reaction or a response. I use this as a daily devotional. I find my peace by holding my peace. For that matter, I have learned when to keep my "my two cents" for the things that count. Voices can transcend generations. They can declare things that have never been seen before. Voices rise and set with the sun. My voice is the keeper of my peace. It heals my soul. It is so amazing for a woman to find her voice and speak for herself. Her voice can lead her to opportunities never before thought possible because someone else would have talked her out of them. A woman finding her speaking voice, and listening to her inner voice –the voice of God—is exhilarating. You will find, like I did, that you already have the peace needed for every situation!

CHAPTER 22

Looking For Love

CHERLYN OLIVER-GERSHAM

As a little girl growing up in New York City, I had many unanswered questions. Learning and becoming a woman was hard. My mother was a functional coke addict who abused us by leaving us alone to raise each other. My sisters and I were forced to survive. I cannot say what I learned about being a woman, but I can say what I know about being a survivor. Out of my mother's marriage to my father came me and my sister. Our younger sister came out from her marriage to our stepfather. It was at that time that we moved around a lot, never knowing where we would be next. We stayed with our mother's friends until we were able to get a place of our own. My great-aunt Dot came and got me during the weekends. She favored me out of all my sisters. My grandmother never wanted us around. I remember going to her house and always hearing her say, "Y'all kids get away with all your barking (coughing)!), but she still kept us on occasion. My aunts favored my older sister; I guess because her skin was lighter than mine and our younger sister. And no one really took to my younger sister. I believe it was because my family did not like my stepfather.

My mother was very abusive to us girls. We were to be seen and not heard. Even if she was wrong, we had to agree with everything she said, or we could expect to be beaten. At about six years old, I remember my mother and stepfather having a fight. We lived in a duplex at that time, so my stepdad asked us to go downstairs. My mother did not agree. She said we were her "three bitches", and we were to listen to her. She made us sit on the couch in birth order so we could watch them continue to fight. She told my stepdad to leave. He could either walk out or be carried out. He picked up a cast iron frying pan and hit my mother upside the head. Without a moment's notice, my mother stabbed him in the gut. I guess he got carried out.

A few years pass by, and I am now a preteen. I was still being abused by my mother, but by this time, I was also molested by my uncle and the maintenance guy. My mother never helped because she never listened. I got into boys early in life because they were the only ones who seemed to want me. I could be anything any man wanted me to be, and this seemed to work for me, so I thought. By the time I was thirteen, boys were the only thing on my mind. They noticed me, they listened to me, and they pretended to care. By this time, my mother moved to the borough where our rich stepdad lived. She finally gave him a son, so I guess her "three little bitches" went out the door. I could not take it anymore. If this was love, it was killing us. My sister tried to commit suicide just to get away from our mother. She survived, but she eventually left home to stay with one of our aunts. On the other hand, I was sent to a group home when I was thirteen. I was dating a boy, and I guess she had me sent away because it was a situation she could not control. I was now in a group home environment with girls I should never have been around.

Only my sisters understood what it was like being raised

in this manner. Without a father of my own, being an abused woman became second nature. Love should not have to hurt, but it did for me. As a growing young woman, I screamed out for help but to no avail. I looked for love in all the wrong places because I never knew what it was. I wanted to come back home, but that did not happen until three years later. After being in thirteen different group homes, I went to a foster home. My foster mother worked, kept me dressed, and made sure I stayed educated. But every Friday, she went to a bar with her female friend and come home drunk and coked up. When she got home, she would pull me out bed and call me the devil. She said I was evil. She almost sounded like my mother. But the one thing I always held on to was my mother's survival rules: 1) never trust a man to do anything for you; 2) always be independent; 3) always be able to provide for yourself, and 4) depend on no one else but yourself. She did raise us to be strong, independent black women; but she left a hole in our hearts. We all have a story to tell, and this one is mine.

I ran to the first man who showed me love. I had "daddy issues," an informal phrase for a woman's psychological challenges resulting from an absent or abnormal relationship with their father, often manifesting in a distrust of, or sexual desire for, men who act as father figures. Go figure. All the men I dealt with were ten to eleven years older than me. I never knew why. By the time I was eighteen, I had literally become a chameleon, I was taught to adapt under anycircumstance. I had my first child, a daughter. I remember wanting kids so bad. Because I never received love, I wanted to create a family that loved me. I had always been full of love and life, but I had no one to share it with. Everybody had an agenda, and it never included loving me. Even though my daughter's father cheated on me, I still married him. Now nineteen years old, I thought I was in love, and that someone loved me. That love led me to have an abortion at five months into my pregnancy. That baby was not his, but he made sure I had his son. He basically beat me every other day for two years. He had me isolated me from my family and friends. The ultimate abuse was my own husband raping me to have babies. He wanted to keep me barefoot and pregnant so no one else would want me.

I made the fateful decision to kill myself, but then I wondered what would happen to my kids. Where would they go? I could not take it anymore. I was twenty-one and eight months pregnant with my third child by rape. I had to get away from that situation so. With his mother's help, we strategically planned my getaway. I went to a domestic violence shelter. One day, I decided to end my pregnancy because of how it came about. So, I ventured out to the abortion clinic with my babies in my double stroller. While walking down the street with tears in my eyes, I heard a voice say, "Stop, turn around. You are not going to do this." I looked around and no one was around me. I kept walking and then the voice spoke again: "Stop, you are not going to do this." What was this? It was the voice of the Lord! He told me that she belonged to him, and that I had to return her to him. Then he told me, "Look up! This is her name!" The Lord stopped me in front of Trinity Baptist Church. It was then that I started my journey with the Lord and learned how to become a woman of God. This was the moment that shifted everything in my life. I am not saying that everything was suddenly alright; in fact, things were about to get harder. But for the first time, I stepped out on faith. I took on a life of faith and leaned on Jesus. This baby was the third, and her name was going to be Trinity. As I said before, I was in a battered women's shelter, but I ended up going back to my husband for a while. My sentimental self was going to get me killed, If you have ever been in my situation, you know how hard it is to venture out on your own at twenty-one years old with three children (all less than three years old) and one on the way. Sometimes we seem to think we cannot make it, or at least this is what we are brainwashed to believe; but God was with me. As he had at the beginning, he helped me through my wrong decisions.

Twenty years pass by and bring me to marriage with my second husband and three more children. Besides this, I had another change in my life. I fell into the mistakes of my past. Drugs. Being with a man who I never loved and did not know how to love me. He was safe. He did not hit me. He did not hang out on the street. He seemed to be a man of God, and he did not mind raising my children with me. There was just one problem: we were unequally yoked. I was advised not to marry him, so when I did, it was not my pastor I disobeyed. It was God. That disobedience brought twelve years of division in my home that eventually led to a separation. In those twelve years, I was not faithful. After this, I did something that I never did. I took a two-year sabbatical to reflect on my wants, needs, desires, and dreams. I spent so many years chameleonizing myself to fit everyone else's needs. I did not know who I was. I continued going to church, knowing and feeling that there was more for me in this life. I never gave up, but I was tired. It was going to take this last experience to turn my lifearound forever. I met someone on the way to church one day. This person would be the one God used to open my eyes for real. I fell so hard for him that it was not funny. And as usual, I thought I was in love. I wondered if I really even knew what love was. God was always the only love I needed, but I spent the next eight years learning that the hard way.

It is now September 2018, where my life seemed to be at the lowest it could possibly be. I started smoking crack with this so-called love who did not love me. He used the goodness in me that I never knew existed. I became severely stricken in my body and became like a vegetable for almost five years. I had two strokes and a heart attack. I had ungrateful children who could not see how I was disappearing right before their eye. The depression got so bad that I did not want to be here anymore. Why was this so hard? Why was this my life? Why did the ones I love hate me? Love does not hurt. Love is not jealous and insecure. It is patient and kind. From the weight of having an abusive mother, relationships with men who were not good for me, my marriages to abusive men, and my own children fighting with me, I was done. I felt like I was cursed for being rebellious and disobedient. I bedded many and was faithful to none. I thought this was my fate.

But God! One day I just dropped to knees after a huge argument with one of my daughters. I was going to end it all in a corner of my room. Instead, I turned to the God I had been running from all my life. I cried and pleaded with the Lord to save me. I did not want to live this way anymore. I did not want to hurt or be hurt anymore. While at a church service, I was refilled with the Holy Ghost. I was renewed, forgiven, and set free. Now it was up to me. I went into the first week of 2019 thinking, "For God I live, and for God I die" Forgetting those men and my kids, I concentrated on my walk with the Lord. and men, and just concentration on the Lord and my walk with him. My overseer told me I was being honored, and I asked her why.

For living? She answered that with a question and said, "You're living for God, right?" And it was done. The ceremony was going to take place on July 29th. I need you to pay close attention to this.

In February 2019, I received a gift bag shaped like a pillowcase. I only had eight dollars to my name. I took a cab home, and when I got there, I opened the gift bag and money flew out of it all around the cab. It felt like I just robbed a bank! Where did this money come from? I was scared to death, but then I heard a voice say, "Owe nothing to no man". This was strange. I received a letter from my landlord saying that I owed rent, but I did not owe anything, I was going to get this business straight. Little did I know it was all taken care of. I rushed home and told my nephew to immediately to pay off whatever debt I had. Later in March, I took a friend of mine to see where I did volunteer and missionary work in a school. It was there that I heard the words that changed life forever and for the better. That voice said, "It's time now to start the church". Many years prior, my bishop told me it was time to start my own church. I paid her no mind about it. I was nowhere near being ready to start a church of my own. But those words came back to me ten years later. I was told to buy a laptop. I was listening and following what God told me to do. One day I am working and just typing away. Before I knew it, I had an entire PowerPoint presentation on the ministry and mission statement. I was amazed and wondered how this happened. Then I heard that voice again, saying, "Now do you know why I gave you that education? Now can you see? I put you in that church so you could see yourself, what you had become. Now that you have truly received deliverance, and your spirit is grieved, you are now ready to receive what I had to give you. I put you in the world to receive the education that would later be used for my glory. I had to pull you out and lay you down because the world was pulling you away from me." I was tears!

The next few months were spent building the ministry. One day in August, I received a call from Arizona, telling me that the home I applied for two years prior was ready. Walking by faith and not by sight, I boarded a plane to Arizona on August 31st, 2019. Other than packing up and giving in my old key, I never want to return to where I left. and other than packing up and giving in my old key will never return to that city. In January 2021, I became a pastor/overseer with Women in Christ Ministries. I worked on a book, and it became a number-one best seller. I became a number-one bestselling author. I got a job with the state of Arizona. To top things off, I received a vision of a man in a dream at the beginning of 2020. I started attending church and one day, that man from my dream walked into church. Where did he come from? And why he was in my dream? I pulled to the side and asked him who he was, and why was he in my dream. As you can imagine, he looked at me like I was crazy and said, "Well I don't know why I was in your dream, miss!" We both laughed and before you know it, we became the best friends.

With me being alone in a new place, he became very convenient. I did not have a car at that time. I was still being restored, so I used a walker. He was extremely helpful. Our friendship grew stronger and stronger. Who would have known we would both be delivered into one another? That could only take place with God. A year passed us by, and we became truly fond of each other. I never knew a love like this. We are both believers of Christ and are equally yoked. Especially important,

God gave me my heart's desire through obedience. I have life partner and a partner in Christ. He is someone who loves me for who I am. Someone I can trust and who trusts me. How is it that I am so blessed, when at one time I was stressed and depressed? I was finally able to let my guard down because I knew God finally had me. For Christmas, we became engaged! WON'T HE DO IT? Now you know what it was like for this woman being a woman. It has been the hardest thing ever. All the confusion, disrespect, and childhood issues can drive you into a world of chaos just to prove you like gold. This is what God did for me. He made me a virtuous Proverbs 31 woman. So, with me taking in the good with the bad, being a woman is wonderful. But becoming an anointed woman of God is better.

CHAPTER 23

Focused On God

JUANITA LEVY

I am a God-focused woman who was born in Brooklyn, New York during the nineteen-sixties. The Merriam-Webster Dictionary definition of a woman is "an adult female person," but my definition of a woman is about knowing who I am, and being focused to obtain what God has in store for me. He taught me how to be caring, consistent, dependable, loving, and trustworthy.

Every day, it is this blessing, honor, and gift of being a woman that I treasure. There is no one on earth like the anointed, appointed woman that God made me before I was in mother's womb. I have always known that I am a one-of-a-kind designer original. The fact that I was designed by the greatest designer in the universe makes me unique. As a woman, I have so many incredible attributes that allow me to shape my life, and the lives of others as well.

Foundation is important. I was one of six children born into the Dowtin dynasty. My first teachers were my father, Saint Dowtin, and my mother, Sarah Dowtin. My parents provided me and my siblings with daily care, direction and guidance. While we grew up, the core of the Dowtin household was built on this scripture: "... as for me and my house, we will serve the Lord" (Joshua 24:15). My parents' marriage was the first love story I ever saw, and it was that kind of relationship I desired to have one day. And let us be honest: we all would love to have true love. It does exist, and the first example we were taught is where God gave the world his only begotten Son (John 3:16).

God's call on my life was recognized in my teenage years. From my parents' instruction, serving God and others came naturally to me (Philippians 2:3-5). It was second nature. My siblings had always been a great source of support in my life, and our hearts were broken when my baby brother (the firstborn brother), Saint Dowtin, was taken from us to be home with the Lord. Another brother, Calvin, helped me a lot then, and from that time forward. But a different kind of help in my life came from my sisters: Jeanette, Jackie and Deborah. My sisters mentored me. They enabled me to become a phenomenal woman and thrive all throughout my life.

It takes a village to raise a child. My village was surrounded with anointed, appointed women sent by God. Their lives of service was pleasing to God, and witnessed by me. The first example was my mother, Sarah Dowtin, who worked faithfully and joyfully in every capacity of service in the body of Christ. But she also showed me how it is always a worthwhile goal to work hard for what I need or want. Failure to plan how to get what I need is a plan for failure. None of us desire not to succeed! We all want to succeed, and we were taught that all things are possible through Christ.

My parents supported and encouraged us to pursue education. A good education could open up many possibilities for achieving the goals we set for our lives (Ecclesiastes 7:12). After one eye examination, I was told I would have to wear glasses. This is where I found out how children can choose to be cruel. Because of my need to wear glasses, I was constantly bullied. I became very self-conscious, but I also realized that my glasses, now a part of me, where essential for me to achieve success in my reading and learning. As I matured over the years, especially in my walk with God, I became very confident about how God made me. I started carrying a mirror with me to remind myself of who he made me to be. I understood that God would not give me any more than I was able to bear.

During the winter of 1984, I was blessed to have my future husband, Frank Levy, find me, just as the Bible tells us: "Whoso findeth a wife findeth a good thing, and obtaineth favour of the LORD" (Proverbs 18:22). Once I became a married woman, all the characteristics of being a good wife came easily. I watched my mother as she did it for years in my childhood home. She definitely led by example, demonstrating in her daily life all the tools a woman could use to achieve success as a wife. Now living my dream of being a wife and maintaining my own home, I experienced joy in being the "woman of the house". At this time in my life, I acquired a job caring for others, which was the goal I set while attending high school. For many women, the next step in their marriage journey is the wonderful gift of becoming a mother. In November 1987, becoming mother to my son, Frank Levy, Jr., was one of the greatest days of my life. I was able to nurture and care for him, and being responsible for this person's well-being is, and will always be, an honor I cherish and love (Luke 1:38).

After several years of marriage, my husband and I decided to end our marriage, but we would continue to care our son. It was not an easy time, but with God on my side, I came through it as a strong and victorious woman who was ready for my next assignment from him (Proverbs 31:10). I continued receiving mentoring from the extraordinary women of Zion in my life: the church mothers of Holy Dove Church. The way these women lived their lives in front of me helped me to know I was going to get through and make it. They served God, the body of Christ, and their communities with joy and excellence. They also demonstrated how the power of prayer works (Matthew 7:7). God orchestrated a circle of fearfully and wonderfully made women to cover me, to encourage me, and to love me through every situation. The strength I gained through these extraordinary women helped me to be able to pour into other women. With God on my side, I have already won!

Each day, I strive to achieve perfection. In 2002, it was time for my brother, Bishop Saint Christopher Zebedee Dowtin, III (BSCZDIII), to spread his wings and open up the Covenant of Hope Church in Brooklyn, New York. Serving under his leadership, I held many positions due to the experience I gained before: missionary, usher, and nurse. They were all positions of service. By my service to God, and through God's word, I have been able to be a good servant. God's word provided all the instruction I needed to guide me through any assignment. In the word of God, I have found all the lessons and knowledge needed to help me live the life of the virtuous woman the world sees today. All glory belongs to God!

By staying in God's word, it allows me to be consistent in walking his way. I rely on his strength every day to fulfill the assignment he has entrusted to me; "I can do all things through Christ which strengtheneth me" (Philippians 4:13). Wherever I go, and whatever I go through, I know God will never leave or forsake me. Because he is reliable, he has taught me how to be a reliable woman. For my family and friends, I am always just a phone call away.

The experiences of the past two years have been amazing, but I have been able to survive. It was not just me, but it was the grace of God. He gives us new grace and mercy each day, and he has allowed us all to still be here. Hallelujah! As I walk with God each day, I know my purpose is to serve him and please him with everything I say and do. My joy and happiness comes from showing my love for people. Through love, it will always be my portion to have a heart after God, and for the things of God.

World history shows how everyone tries to leave their mark on the world. Our legacies are our family and children. Through my son, and his children's mother Pamlita, I was able to become a grandmother to their twins, son Adrian, and their daughter Adriana. Through experience I have acquired over my life, I can share my tools with these two future world changers. I really enjoy the lessons that I share with my oldest granddaughter Adrianne. By having a relationship with God, and by serving him, I have learned what things are important in a relationship. Doing things his way ensures success in all of my life's relationships. I am very blessed to have great friendships with several women. As we deal with this new "normal", we share how we maneuver through our daily life challenges. My circle of strong women sent by God has enabled me to receive encouragement, knowledge, love, understanding and wisdom. There is always strength in numbers, and we are always stronger together than if we were divided (2 Corinthians 13:11).

I make a special mention of my cousin, Apostle Cheryl Wade, has been a spiritual influence in my life. The life she lived before me, my family, and the world, has been a blessing to and for us all. My faith comes first, and my family and friends will always be dear to me. Family members have been some of my greatest cheerleaders. And not to be forgotten is my church family, made up of people who are God's gifts to us to help us know that ALL things are possible through Christ our Lord and Savior. God strengthens us from day to day. His love will always cover us and the challenges we face in our daily life journey. Through love, there is nothing my biological and church family would not do for me, or for each other (Philippians 4:13). Our journeys are all connected through Christ. Please be encouraged to know that your labor is, and will never be, in vain (1 Corinthians 15:58).

CHAPTER 24

My Journey From Addiction

SHIRL JONES

I was born in New York City. My parents were from a small town in North Carolina. From the age of five, I grew up in the Jehovah's Witness lifestyle. I had one sibling, a brother, and we lived a very sheltered life. I was not allowed to have many friends. My brother and I did not have much of a chance for friendships because with the lifestyle our parents had us living, all we were supposed to do was serve God and do nothing else. We still had a good childhood, and my brother was my best friend. When I was about sixteen years old, there was a boy who I really liked, and I told my brother. I thought he would keep my secret, but he told our dad!

It was 1984, when I was eighteen years old. That year, I lost my dad. It was such a sad situation to have to deal with, but God got us through it. I had no idea that a few months later, things would begin to look up when I would meet the man who became my husband and the father of my three children. As soon as things started to look up, another death happened. On August 7th, 1986, I lost my mother. Even though this just happened, I married my husband on October 18th, 1986. I thought we would be together forever, but I was very wrong. My life changed, and I lost myself. I was in depression, and I did not know how to handle it. It was at this time that I was introduced to a life of drugs, alcohol, and domestic violence.

A few years later, on June 17th, 1988, I lost my best friend. My brother was tragically killed when he was hit by a New York City fire truck. He was only nineteen. I was alone in the world, or so I thought. I gave birth to my first child during this time. I was still drinking and doing drugs to escape the pain of all the loss that I had in my life. I tried to get out from the abuse I suffered, but it was hard. I stayed because I wanted my family together, so the abuse continued for years.

One day I met an awesome woman of God, Cherlyn Oliver, who is now my pastor. I still remember the day that I met her. A friend of mine, who knew I had just lost my husband on January 26, 1996, had been trying to get me out the house. Instead, she invited a missionary from her church to come talk with me and pray with me. She came and did just that, and not much later, I ended up attending the same church where we were inseparable.

Years had passed us by and in 2008, I met a man while I worked as a security guard at the airport. I thought this relationship was going to be a good one, but the enemy came in. Again, I started going through the same mess the Lord delivered me from before. I still attended church, but I backslide and began drinking again. The abuse started again too, but I kept going to church. I endured this for years, and then in 2014, the Lord spoke to me and told me it was time to go. I had no idea what he meant, but he used my baby daughter and my son-in-law to make it happen. Even though I had been abused for a long time, leaving was not an easy situation. I stopped doing drugs and drinking alcohol, so to God be the glory!

The Lord began to heal me. He told me that I am a strong woman. Being a woman means that I have strength, and I thank the Lord for saving me by his strength. Being a woman means I had to be a protector for my children. Being a woman means there will be times that my feelings are all over the place. Being a woman meant when I really wanted to leave a bad situation, I had to learn to listen to God. He is in control. He spoke to me, and I obeyed him so I could begin the process of healing from a life of pain and disappointment. To God be the glory! What I needed was patience, strength, and the will to do as I was instructed.

Being a woman means I will cry when I am sad. I did a lot of crying as I went through the pain in my life. Little did I know that my tears were prayers to be heard by God. He heard my cries and my pleas. He rescued me from all my problems. God had a plan for my life. I had an issue with trust, but God helped me with this. I trusted God to give me the help I needed, but I understood that he had to move me to a place where I would be safe. A place where I would have no distractions. A place where I could learn to serve him. Being a woman means I can deal with problems that I think that I cannot handle at first. God taught me that as long as I trust him, he will place no more on me than I can bear. He will guide me through any problems that I face and anything that might come my way.

Being a woman means that we deal with our physical pain. Childbirth is the most painful thing any woman can go through, and I went through it three times. And then there are other things our bodies and minds go through, like hot flashes, emotions going overboard, and our mood swings. Being a woman is not always easy, but to God be the glory! In becoming a mother, I dealt with the pain of worrying about my children, always wanting to make sure they had everything they needed. But on the other side of this, I had to deal with my own issues. Being a woman does not mean I am superhuman. Sometimes I need help. Through the strength of the Lord, I can accomplish things I want to do and face any hardship in life.

Even though I love being a woman, as I said before, there are times when I want to do a lot of crying. But the God I serve gives me comfort whenever those times come about. Being a woman means that sometimes I have to deal with heartbreak, but the God I serve is the mender of broken hearts. I may have to cry sometimes, but it is alright. God is the One who wipes away every tear I shed. Being a woman, I learned how to guard my heart. God showed me that when I guard my heart, I am treating it as a precious thing. I am protecting it from corruption. His word says that out of the abundance of the heart, the mouth speaks (Matthew 12:34).

I give honor and praise to God for creating and molding me to be the woman I am today. He kept me. He protected my children. When I was being abused through domestic violence, and even when I abused myself, he kept me. I did not know how to love myself, and I thought no one else could love me. Or so I thought. When I was depressed, I did not know it, but God revealed it to me. Even though I knew what to do and how to do it, depression took my strength and motivation to execute what I knew I had to do. I realize it was God who gave me the strength and will to live again. I no longer feel sheltered or immobilized anymore. Many years ago, I did not enjoy being a woman because of what I went through, but now, all glory be to God!

I love being a woman. I realize that being the woman who God created me to be is amazingly awesome. Being a woman means I am a warrior of God, and a daughter of the King. I am worthy of love and respect. I am royalty, and my royalty comes from being a daughter of the King, and a joint heir with Jesus Christ. I have been given keys to the kingdom of God to do God's work on earth. If you asked me eight years ago about what being a woman meant to me, I would have told you that it was very hard, but I now know I was created for purpose. I am blessed in how God created me. When I wake up, I thank God for giving me strength and courage to go on. He gave me his word. So many women have lost their trust. I know, because I was one of them. I put my trust in the Lord so I could become a renewed woman. Being a woman, I know for myself that God is my way maker. It means I can trust God and know he can change things in my life, just like he changed my life. I said it enough times already, but I cannot say it enough. God strengthened me to go through hell and back. Unless I told them, no one would even know just from looking at me. Being a woman with responsibility and growth comes from within. As royalty, I will not settle for anything less than what I deserve. I thank the Lord for healing me and bringing out my womanhood. When God created me, he created a masterpiece.

CHAPTER 25

From Loneliness To Wholeness

KRISTINE JOHN

God has been the author of my life, even in times of uncertainty. It has been my testimony over the years that God is faithful, and has been the One I ran to throughout my hurt and pain. He was there when I was physically, emotionally, and spiritually broken. I take this opportunity to tell my testimony. Through, and because of, my educational journey over the years, I lived in a painful world of loneliness. But thanks be to God, that journey led me from being an underachieving high school student to one who would become a PhD in the sciences.

Raised in the town of New Amsterdam, Guyana, South America, I came from a family of four children, where my mother was a well-known teacher and disciplinarian. She always encouraged us to work hard, despite the occasional struggles she and my father had in their marriage. By the time I was ready to take the Common Entrance national examination to move forward to secondary school, my mother (who was also a Common Entrance Teacher), worked with me at home. I focused and worked hard to pass. When the results came out, I passed so well that I was able to go to the top regional school. This brought tears to my mother's eyes because things were quite challenging for us as a family. Even though this happened, I began to struggle when I got there. For most of my years in high school, I moved from one level to the next on conditional promotion. Most of my August holidays were spent in summer school. At that time, I was an active member of my local church Sunday school and youth fellowship. I remember praying before I wrote examinations, asking God to intervene so that I could pass my end-term examinations. God was faithful, and from first form to third form, from level to level, I was promoted. Even though the promotions were conditional, I was able to move forward to upper secondary school.

On my entrance at that level (fourth form), years of preparation for the Caribbean Regional examinations began. I repeated the fourth form because the examination determined that I was not ready for the fifth form. However, when I took the CXC (now CSEC) examination, I passed seven out of nine subjects and was given the "Most Surprising CXC Student" award at high school graduation. I was ready to go to college, but our parents could not afford to send three children at the same time. So, I waited a year until two of my siblings graduated. The next year (1997), I enrolled at the university as an undergraduate student with a geography major. By the second year, I took on a biology as a second major. This double major program was very heavy, but my faith in God allowed me to manage twelve courses per semester for two years.

It was 1999, and I was twenty-one years old at that time. Tragically, my eldest brother died in a car accident at the beginning of my second year of university, and that is when life became difficult for me and our mother. My other brother became abusive, and I was told that this was due to him grieving over the loss of our brother who died. Our mother had gotten depressed because of his behavior, and since my other sister left home, I wound up having to take care of her. This responsibility was a huge weight. It took a huge toll on my grades because I was still carrying heavy course loads. There were many times when I called home and my mother just broke down in tears because of my brother cursing her out. Despite my course load, I still managed. I failed only one course during the semester when my brother died. God kept my head above water so that I could pass all my classes, despite the challenges I faced at home.

I have to mention that one week after my brother's funeral, out of a place of grief and mourning, I gave up my virginity. It began a period of fornication that continued for the next year. In fact, I was so unhappy fornicating because I knew God was not happy with me for what I was doing. I wrote him long letters and told him so. I wrote about my uneasiness with being a fornicator and how I thought God viewed me. And then I met a guy who showed a different kind of interest in me. I immediately got the strength to leave fornicating relationships.

When I entered my final year in the double major program, I was encouraged to drop one major and complete my degree majoring in the other. Due to so many family burdens, this was the second time I was advised to do so. I did so and managed to graduate, but I later returned to try and finish a degree for the major I dropped before. I graduated with another degree. I later tried to pursue a master's degree, but my GPAs for the two degrees were not very high. Before all this, I tried to use wisdom by registering for three post-graduate courses while I was finishing the final year of my second-degree curriculum. If I passed those courses, they would have allowed me to gain a post-graduate diploma.

The fact that I did this led to a registrar office investigation. I was sent a strongly worded letter from the registrar. They were not being pleased that I tried to enroll in two programs at the same time. I was later described as the "crook" of the University, along with other sorts of names. The university administration placed lots of blame on me, claiming that I tried to manipulate the system. But what did God do for me? I ended up getting that post-graduate diploma with distinction, and that same year, I received a Commonwealth Scholarship to pursue a Master of Science degree in the United Kingdom. But God!

The Commonwealth Scholarship came with a cost. This was a time in my life where I trusted God with every inch of myself. After I had the interview for the scholarship, I felt like it went so well that I would get it. Not only did I believe God had given me the scholarship, but no one could tell me it was not so. Not even those who were close to me and screamed at me for believing what they thought not to be true. It did not matter. I knew in my heart that God gave it to me. My faith was much increased. Because of all God brought me through, I knew him for myself. Without seeing it, I knew in my heart that the scholarship was mine. When I received and showed proof of the scholarship award to the administration of the university that scapegoated me, they were astonished by my hard work.

In 2005, the next stop along my journey was spending a year in the UK to complete my Master of Science degree. For whatever reason (only God knows), I was told that I was "mad." I was laughed at and ridiculed. At the completion of that degree program, I applied to the PhD program at the University of Nottingham. I was only given a partial tuition scholarship, and I took it because I was determined. Even though I got into the program, I contemplated suicide because of all the ridicule I got from people I considered as family and friends. This was a very trying time in my life. By the end of that first year at Nottingham, I had a serious mental breakdown, and was admitted into a mental institution. I was homeless at that time because the job I had as a cleaner could not pay my bills. I later returned to Guyana and showed up at the university once again, but this time as a lecturer.

Seven years after returning from the UK, and after several attempts to get admitted to a PhD program in the US, I was admitted to the CUNY Graduate Center's Earth and Environmental Sciences program. This time, I was fully funded for five years. I received tuition and a stipend because I taught as a graduate assistant at Brooklyn College, where my studies were based. In my fifth year of study, I had a physical injury that slowed me down. I broke my kneecap and had surgery, but God healed me. It took me seven and a half years to complete my PhD coursework, but I got through it.

The next year (2018), I met Elton John. We got into a relationship that ended up with us getting married, however, the week after he proposed to me, I found out I was pregnant. This occurred after our first sexual experience before getting married. We got married a month later on November 24th, 2018. Our son Pharez was born on July 12th, 2019, but after this, I had a severe case of postpartum depression. For the first time in my life, I was not on the receiving end of the cursing line. I was handing them out to all the people who hurt me over the years. This resulted with me being admitted to a mental institution—again—and spending five days there before returning home to my husband and young son. Since the time of this breakdown, I have been using prescribed psychiatric medications. Their presence has been a constant factor in my daily life, and for that, I am seeking God for freedom and deliverance.

In all this, I am a testimony that God is faithful. Despite the trials and testing he brought me through, I know he has greater things in store. Romans 8:31 has proven true to me and my family: "What shall we then say to these things? If God be for us, who can be against us?" I want to thank God for keeping me throughout my life, and for placing people in my life who love me. If God could keep me, he can keep you too!

AWESOME WOMEN ON THE MOVE PRESENTS...

WHAT IT IS LIKE BEING A

Dr. Tenaria Drummond-Smith

AWESOME WOMEN ON THE MOVE

Products

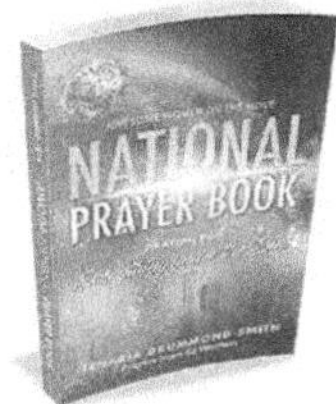

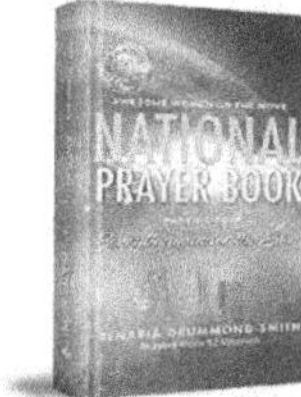

amazon.com BARNES&NOBLE.com www.bn.com Walmart TARGET

Connect With Us

@AwesomeWomenOnTheMove

@AWOTMSocialMedia
@TinnySmith7

tenariadrummondsmith@yahoo.com

www.ingramcontent.com/pod-product-compliance
Lightning Source LLC
Chambersburg PA
CBHW071810190726
48292CB00008B/2787